PERFORMANCE MANAGEMENT

PERFORMANCE MANAGEMENT

KEY STRATEGIES AND PRACTICAL GUIDELINES

3RD EDITION

Michael Armstrong

KOGAN PAGE

London and Philadelphia

Publisher's note

Every possible effort has been made to ensure that the information contained in this book is accurate at the time of going to press, and the publishers and author cannot accept responsibility for any errors or omissions, however caused. No responsibility for loss or damage occasioned to any person acting, or refraining from action, as a result of the material in this publication can be accepted by the editor, the publisher or the author.

First published in Great Britain and the United States in 1994 by Kogan Page Limited
Second edition 2000
Third edition 2006
Reprinted 2006, 2007, 2008

120 Pentonville Road
London N1 9JN
United Kingdom
www.koganpage.com

525 South 4th Street, #241
Philadelphia PA 19147
USA

ISBN-10   0 7494 4537 8
ISBN-13   978 0 7494 4537 9

British Library Cataloguing-in-Publication Data

A CIP record for this book is available from the British Library.

Library of Congress Cataloging-in-Publication Data

Armstrong, Michael, 1928–
   Performance management : key strategies and practical guidelines / Michael Armstrong.— 3rd ed.
    p. cm.
   Includes bibliographical references and index.
   ISBN 0-7494-4537-8
   1. Employees—Rating of. 2. Performance standards. 3. Performance. I. Title.
HF5549.5.R3A758 2006
658.3′125—dc22
                  2005021779

Typeset by Saxon Graphics Ltd, Derby
Printed and bound in India by Replika Press Pvt Ltd

Contents

1

The basis of performance management

In this chapter the nature, aims, characteristics, concerns and guiding principles of performance management are described. In addition, the differences between performance appraisal and performance management are examined and reference is made to the views of a selection of practitioners on performance management. The chapter concludes with a summary of the process of performance management, which is considered more comprehensively in Chapter 2.

PERFORMANCE MANAGEMENT DEFINED

Performance management can be defined as a systematic process for improving organizational performance by developing the performance of individuals and teams. It is a means of getting better results from the organization, teams and individuals by understanding and managing performance within an agreed framework of planned goals, standards and competence requirements. Processes exist for establishing shared understanding about what *is* to be achieved, and for managing and developing people in a way that increases the probability that it *will* be achieved in the short and longer term. It is owned and driven by line management.

Other definitions are:

▌ Performance management is: 'The development of individuals with competence and commitment, working towards the achievement of shared meaningful objectives within an organisation which supports and encourages their achievement' (Lockett, 1).

▌ 'Performance management is managing the business' (Mohrman and Mohrman, 2).

▌ Performance management is: the process of 'Directing and supporting employees to work as effectively and efficiently as possible in line with the needs of the organisation' (Walters, 3).

▌ 'Performance management is a strategic and integrated approach to delivering sustained success to organisations by improving the performance of the people who work in them and by developing the capabilities of teams and individual contributors' (Armstrong and Baron, 4).

AIMS OF PERFORMANCE MANAGEMENT

The overall aim of performance management is to establish a high-performance culture in which individuals and teams take responsibility for the continuous improvement of business processes and for their own skills and contributions within a framework provided by effective leadership. Its key purpose is to focus people on doing the right things by achieving goal clarity.

Specifically, performance management is about aligning individual objectives to organizational objectives and ensuring that individuals uphold corporate core values. It provides for expectations to be defined and agreed in terms of role responsibilities and accountabilities (expected to do), skills (expected to have) and behaviours (expected to be). The aim is to develop the capacity of people to meet and exceed expectations and to achieve their full potential to the benefit of themselves and the organization. Importantly, performance management is concerned with ensuring that the support and guidance people need to develop and improve are readily available.

The following are the aims of performance management as expressed by a variety of organizations (source: *IRS Employment Trends*, 1 August 2003, pp 12–19):

▌ Empowering, motivating and rewarding employees to do their best (*Armstrong World Industries*).

▌ Focusing employees' tasks on the right things and doing them right. Aligning everyone's individual goals to the goals of the organization (*Eli Lilly & Co*).

▌ Proactively managing and resourcing performance against agreed accountabilities and objectives (*ICI Paints*).

▌ Linking job performance to the achievement of the council's medium-term corporate strategy and service plans (*Leicestershire County Council*).

▌ The alignment of personal/individual objectives with team, department/divisional and corporate plans. The presentation of objectives with clearly defined goals/targets using measures, both soft and numeric. The monitoring of performance and tasking of continuous action as required (*Macmillan Cancer Relief*).

▌ All individuals being clear about what they need to achieve and expected standards, and how that contributes to the overall success of the organization; receiving regular, fair, accurate feedback and coaching to stretch and motivate them to achieve their best (*Marks & Spencer Financial Services*).

▌ Systematic approach to organizational performance aligning individual accountabilities to organizational targets and activity (*Royal Berkshire and Battle Hospitals NHS Trust*).

▌ The process and behaviours by which managers manage the performance of their people to deliver a high-achieving organization (*Standard Chartered Bank*).

▌ Maximizing the potential of individuals and teams to benefit themselves and the organization, focusing on achievement of their objectives (*West Bromwich Building Society*).

CHARACTERISTICS OF PERFORMANCE MANAGEMENT

Performance management is a planned process of which the primary elements are agreement, measurement, feedback, positive reinforcement and dialogue. It is concerned with measuring outputs in the shape of delivered performance compared with expectations expressed as objectives. In this respect, it focuses on targets, standards and performance measures or indicators. It is based on the agreement of role requirements, objectives and performance improvement and personal development plans. It provides the setting for ongoing dialogues about performance, which involves the joint and continuing review of achievements against objectives, requirements and plans.

But it is also concerned with inputs and values. The inputs are the knowledge, skills and behaviours required to produce the expected results. Developmental needs are identified by defining these requirements and assessing the extent to which the expected levels of performance have been achieved through the effective use of knowledge and skills and through appropriate behaviour that upholds core values.

Performance management is a continuous and flexible process that involves managers and those whom they manage acting as partners within a framework that sets out how they can best work together to achieve the required results. It is based on the principle of management by contract and agreement rather than management by command. It relies on consensus and cooperation rather than control or coercion.

Performance management focuses on future performance planning and improvement rather than on retrospective performance appraisal. It functions as a continuous and evolutionary process, in which performance improves over time; and provides the basis for regular and frequent dialogues between managers and individuals about performance and development needs. It is mainly concerned with individual performance but it can also be applied to teams. The focus is on development, although performance management is an important part of the reward system through the provision of feedback and recognition and the identification of opportunities for growth. It may be associated with performance- or contribution-related pay but its developmental aspects are much more important.

DEVELOPMENTS IN PERFORMANCE MANAGEMENT

Extensive research carried out in the UK and USA has established that new perspectives on performance management have emerged with the following characteristics:

▮ an emphasis on front-end planning rather than back-end review;

▮ a broader definition of performance that focuses on more than narrowly defined job responsibilities;

▌ an emphasis on ongoing dialogue rather than forms and rating scales;

▌ the recognition that there are many factors contributing to performance outcomes.

CONCERNS OF PERFORMANCE MANAGEMENT

The following are the main concerns of performance management:

▌ *Concern with outputs, outcomes, process and inputs.* Performance management is concerned with outputs (the achievement of results) and outcomes (the impact made on performance). But it is also concerned with the processes required to achieve these results (competencies) and the inputs in terms of capabilities (knowledge, skill and competence) expected from the teams and individuals involved.

▌ *Concern with planning.* Performance management is concerned with planning ahead to achieve future success. This means defining expectations expressed as objectives and in business plans.

▌ *Concern with measurement and review.* 'If you can't measure it you can't manage it.' Performance management is concerned with the measurement of results and with reviewing progress towards achieving objectives as a basis for action.

▌ *Concern with continuous improvement.* Concern with continuous improvement is based on the belief that continually striving to reach higher and higher standards in every part of the organization will provide a series of incremental gains that will build superior performance. This means clarifying what organizational, team and individual effectiveness look like and taking steps to ensure that those defined levels of effectiveness are achieved. As Armstrong and Murlis (5) wrote, this involves: 'Establishing a culture in which managers, individuals and groups take responsibility for the continuous improvement of business processes and of their own skills, competencies and contribution.'

▌ *Concern with continuous development.* Performance management is concerned with creating a culture in which organizational and individual learning and development is a continuous process. It provides means for the integration of learning and work so that everyone learns from the successes and challenges inherent in their day-to-day activities.

▊ *Concern for communication.* Performance management is concerned with communication. This is done by creating a climate in which a continuing dialogue between managers and the members of their teams takes place to define expectations and share information on the organization's mission, values and objectives. This establishes mutual understanding of what *is* to be achieved and a framework for managing and developing people to ensure that it *will* be achieved (Armstrong and Murlis, 5).

▊ *Concern for stakeholders.* Performance management is concerned with satisfying the needs and expectations of all the organization's stakeholders – owners, management, employees, customers, suppliers and the general public. In particular, employees are treated as partners in the enterprise whose interests are respected, whose opinions are sought and listened to, and who are encouraged to contribute to the formulation of objectives and plans for their team and for themselves. Performance management should respect the needs of individuals and teams as well as those of the organization, recognizing that they will not necessarily coincide.

▊ *Concern for fairness and transparency.* Four ethical principles that should govern the operation of the performance management process have been suggested by Winstanley and Stuart-Smith (6). These are:
  - respect for the individual;
  - mutual respect;
  - procedural fairness;
  - transparency of decision making.

UNDERSTANDING PERFORMANCE MANAGEMENT

There are five issues that need to be considered to obtain a full understanding of performance management:

1. the meaning of performance;
2. the significance of values;
3. the meaning of alignment;
4. managing expectations;
5. the significance of discretionary behaviour.

The meaning of performance

Performance is often defined simply in output terms – the achievement of quantified objectives. But performance is a matter not only of what people achieve but how they achieve it. The *Oxford English Dictionary* confirms this by including the phrase 'carrying out' in its definition of performance: 'The accomplishment, execution, carrying out, working out of anything ordered or undertaken.' High performance results from appropriate behaviour, especially discretionary behaviour, and the effective use of the required knowledge, skills and competencies. Performance management must examine how results are attained because this provides the information necessary to consider what needs to be done to improve those results.

The concept of performance has been expressed by Brumbach (7) as follows: 'Performance means both behaviours and results. Behaviours emanate from the performer and transform performance from abstraction to action. Not just the instruments for results, behaviours are also outcomes in their own right – the product of mental and physical effort applied to tasks – and can be judged apart from results.' This definition of performance leads to the conclusion that when managing performance both inputs (behaviour) and outputs (results) need to be considered. It is not a question of simply considering the achievement of targets as used to happen in management-by-objectives schemes. Competence factors need to be included in the process. This is the so-called 'mixed model' of performance management, which covers the achievement of expected levels of competence as well as objective setting and review.

Performance management and values

Performance is about upholding the values of the organization – 'living the values' (an approach to which much importance is attached at Standard Chartered Bank). This is an aspect of behaviour but it focuses on what people do to realize core values such as concern for quality, concern for people, concern for equal opportunity and operating ethically. It means converting espoused values into values in use: ensuring that the rhetoric becomes reality.

The meaning of alignment

One of the most fundamental purposes of performance management is to align individual and organizational objectives. This means that every-thing people do at work leads to outcomes that further the achievement of organizational goals. This purpose was well expressed by Fletcher (8) who wrote: 'The real concept of performance management is associated with an approach to creating a shared vision of the purpose and aims of the organisation, helping each employee understand and recognise their part in contributing to them, and in so doing, manage and enhance the performance of both individuals and the organisation.'

Alignment can be attained by a cascading process so that objectives flow down from the top and at each level team or individual objectives are defined in the light of higher-level goals. But it should also be a bottom-up process, individuals and teams being given the opportunity to formulate their own goals within the framework provided by the defined overall purpose, strategy and values of the organization. Objectives should be *agreed*, not set, and this agreement should be reached through the open dialogues that take place between managers and individuals throughout the year. In other words, this needs to be seen as a partnership in which responsibility is shared and mutual expectations are defined.

Managing expectations

Performance management is essentially about the management of expectations. It creates a shared understanding of what is required to improve performance and how this will be achieved by clarifying and agreeing what people are expected to do and how they are expected to behave and uses these agreements as the basis for measurement, review and the preparation of plans for performance improvement and development.

Performance management and discretionary behaviour

Performance management is concerned with the encouragement of productive discretionary behaviour. As defined by Purcell and his team at Bath University School of Management (9), 'Discretionary behaviour refers to the choices that people make about how they carry out their work and the amount of effort, care, innovation and productive behaviour they display. It is the difference between people just doing a job and people doing a great job.' Purcell and his team, while researching the relationship between HR practice and business performance, noted that 'the experience of success seen in performance outcomes help reinforce positive attitudes'.

GUIDING PRINCIPLES OF PERFORMANCE MANAGEMENT

Egan (10) proposes the following guiding principles for performance management:

Most employees want direction, freedom to get their work done, and encouragement not control. The performance management system should be a control system only by exception. The solution is to make it a collaborative development system in two ways. First, the entire performance management process – coaching, counselling, feedback, tracking, recognition, and so forth – should encourage development. Ideally, team members grow and develop through these interactions. Second, when managers and team members ask what they need to be able to do to do bigger and better things, they move to strategic development.

PERFORMANCE APPRAISAL AND PERFORMANCE MANAGEMENT

It is sometimes assumed that performance appraisal is the same thing as performance management. But there are significant differences. Performance appraisal can be defined as the formal assessment and rating of individuals by their managers at, usually, an annual review meeting. In contrast performance management is a continuous and much wider, more comprehensive and more natural process of management that clarifies mutual expectations, emphasizes the support role of managers who are expected to act as coaches rather than judges and focuses on the future.

Performance appraisal has been discredited because too often it has been operated as a top-down and largely bureaucratic system owned by the HR department rather than by line managers. It was often backward looking, concentrating on what had gone wrong, rather than looking forward to future development needs. Performance appraisal schemes existed in isolation. There was little or no link between them and the needs of the business. Line managers have frequently rejected performance appraisal schemes as being time consuming and irrelevant. Employees have resented the superficial nature with which appraisals have been conducted by managers who lack the skills required, tend to be biased and are simply going through the motions. As Armstrong and Murlis (5) assert, performance appraisal too often degenerated into 'a dishonest annual ritual'. The differences between them as summed up by Armstrong and Baron (4) are set out in Table 1.1.

Table 1.1 Performance appraisal compared with performance management

Performance appraisal	Performance management
Top-down assessment	Joint process through dialogue
Annual appraisal meeting	Continuous review with one or more formal reviews
Use of ratings	Ratings less common
Monolithic system	Flexible process
Focus on quantified objectives	Focus on values and behaviours as well as objectives
Often linked to pay	Less likely to be a direct link to pay
Bureaucratic – complex paperwork	Documentation kept to a minimum
Owned by the HR department	Owned by line managers

VIEWS ON PERFORMANCE MANAGEMENT

The research conducted by the CIPD in 2004 (11) elicited the following views from practitioners about performance management:

▌ 'We expect line managers to recognise it [performance management] as a useful contribution to the management of their teams rather than a chore' (*Centrica*).

▌ 'Managing performance is about coaching, guiding, motivating and rewarding colleagues to help unleash potential and improve organisational performance. Where it works well it is built on excellent leadership and high quality coaching relationships between managers and teams' (*Halifax BOS*).

▌ 'Performance management is designed to ensure that what we do is guided by our values and is relevant to the purposes of the organisation' (*Scottish Parliament*).

The research conducted by the CIPD in 1997 (4) obtained the following additional views from practitioners about performance management:

1. 'A management tool which helps managers to manage.'

2. 'Driven by corporate purpose and values.'

3. 'To obtain solutions that work.'

4. 'Only interested in things you can do something about and get a visible improvement.'

5. 'Focus on changing behaviour rather than paperwork.'

6. 'It's about how we manage people – it's not a system.'

7. 'Performance management is what managers do: a natural process of management.'

8. 'Based on accepted principles but operates flexibly.'

9. 'Focus on development not pay.'

10. 'Success depends on what the organisation is and needs to be in its performance culture.'

PERFORMANCE MANAGEMENT AND THE PSYCHOLOGICAL CONTRACT

A psychological contract is a system of beliefs that encompasses the actions employees believe are expected of them and what response they expect in return from their employer. As described by Guest *et al* (12), 'It is concerned with assumptions, expectations, promises and mutual obligations.' Rousseau (13) noted that psychological contracts are 'promissory and reciprocal, offering a commitment to some behaviour on the part of the employee, in return for some action on the part of the employer (usually payment)'.

A positive psychological contract is one in which both parties – the employee and the employer, the individual and the manager – agree on mutual expectations and pursue courses of action that provide for those expectations to be realized. As Guest *et al* (12) remarked: 'A positive psychological contract is worth taking seriously because it is strongly linked to higher commitment to the organisation, higher employee satisfaction and better employment relations.' Performance management has an important part to play in developing a positive psychological contract.

Performance management processes can help to clarify the psychological contract and make it more positive by:

▌ providing a basis for the joint agreement and definition of roles;

▌ communicating expectations in the form of targets, standards of performance, behavioural requirements (competencies) and upholding core values;

▌ obtaining agreement on the contribution both parties (the manager and the individual) have to make to getting the results expected;

▌ defining the level of support to be exercised by managers;

▌ providing rewards that reinforce the messages about expectations;

▌ giving employees opportunities at performance review discussions to clarify points about their work.

THE PROCESS OF PERFORMANCE MANAGEMENT

Performance management should be regarded as a flexible *process*, not as a 'system'. The use of the term 'system' implies a rigid, standardized and bureaucratic approach, which is inconsistent with the concept of performance management as a flexible and evolutionary, albeit coherent, process that is applied by managers working with their teams in accordance with the circumstances in which they operate. As such, it involves managers and those whom they manage acting as partners, but within a framework that sets out how they can best work together. This framework has to reduce the degree to which performance management is a top-down affair and it has to be congruent with the way in which the organization functions. Performance management has to fit process-based and flexible organizations. In these circumstances, which are increasingly the norm, it has to replace the type of appraisal system that only fits a hierarchical and bureaucratic organization.

The processes of performance management consist of:

▌ *Planning*: agreeing objectives and competence requirements and producing performance agreements and performance improvement and personal development plans.

▌ *Acting*: carrying out the activities required to achieve objectives and plans.

▌ *Monitoring*: checking on progress in achieving objectives.

▌ *Reviewing*: assessing progress and achievements so that action plans can be prepared and agreed.

These processes are described in the next chapter.

REFERENCES

1 Lockett, J (1992) *Effective Performance Management*, Kogan Page, London
2 Mohrman, A M and Mohrman, S A (1995) Performance management is 'running the business', *Compensation and Benefits Review*, July–August, pp 69–75
3 Walters, M (1995) *The Performance Management Handbook*, Institute of Personnel and Development, London
4 Armstrong, M and Baron, A (1998) *Performance Management: The new realities*, Institute of Personnel and Development, London
5 Armstrong, M and Murlis, H (1994) *Reward Management*, Kogan Page, London
6 Winstanley, D and Stuart-Smith, K (1996) Policing performance: the ethics of performance management, *Personnel Review*, **25** (6), pp 66–84
7 Brumbach, G B (1988) Some ideas, issues and predictions about performance management, *Public Personnel Management*, Winter, pp 387–402
8 Fletcher, C (1993) *Appraisal: Routes to improved performance*, Institute of Personnel and Development, London
9 Purcell, J et al (2003) *Understanding the People and Performance Link: Unlocking the black box*, CIPD, London
10 Egan, G (1995) A clear path to peak performance, *People Management*, 18 May, pp 34–37
11 Armstrong, M and Baron, A (2005) *Managing Performance: Performance management in action*, Chartered Institute of Personnel and Development, London
12 Guest, D E et al (1996) *The State of the Psychological Contract in Employment*, Institute of Personnel and Development, London
13 Rousseau, D M (1988) The construction of climate in organizational research, in *International Review of Industrial and Organizational Psychology*, ed L C Cooper and I Robertson, Wiley, Chichester

2

The process of performance management

In this chapter, performance management is first considered as a normal process of management and next described as a cycle and a sequence of activities before modelling how it works. The main performance activities are then defined and the chapter ends with examples of performance management models from different organizations.

PERFORMANCE MANAGEMENT AS A PROCESS OF MANAGEMENT

Performance management is a natural process of management. As defined by the total quality expert William Deming (1) it consists of these basic activities:

- *Plan* – decide what to do and how to do it.
- *Act* – carry out the work needed to implement the plan.
- *Monitor* – carry out continuous checks on what is being done and measure outcomes in order to assess progress in implementing the plan.

▮ *Review* – consider what has been achieved and, in the light of this, establish what more needs to be done and any corrective action required if performance is not in line with the plan.

This sequence of activities can be expressed as a continuous cycle as shown in Figure 2.1.

THE PERFORMANCE MANAGEMENT CYCLE

Performance management can be described as a continuous self-renewing cycle as illustrated in Figure 2.2, which follows the plan–act–monitor–review sequence as described above.

THE PERFORMANCE MANAGEMENT SEQUENCE

The sequence of processes carried out in this cycle and the likely outcomes are illustrated in Figure 2.3.

HOW PERFORMANCE MANAGEMENT WORKS

The basis upon which performance management works as a continuous process is illustrated in Figure 2.4.

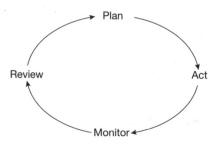

Figure 2.1   The management cycle

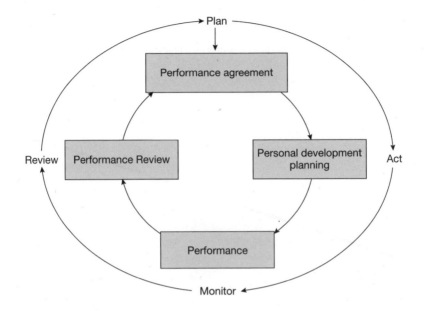

Figure 2.2   The performance management cycle

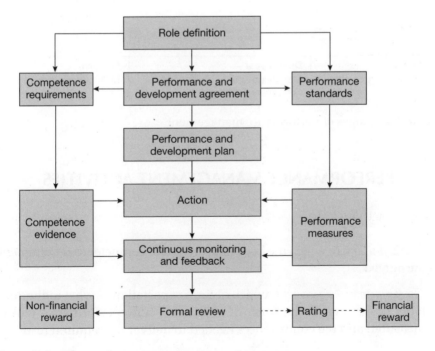

Figure 2.3   The performance management sequence

High performance

• Reinforce through recognition (financial and non-financial, praise, additional responsibility)

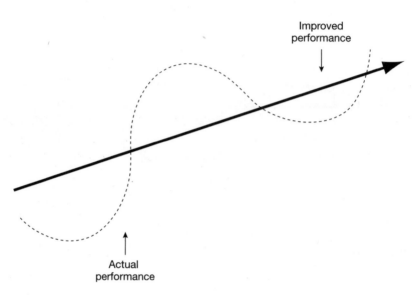

Start year	During year	End year
Performance agreement	Monitoring and review against performance agreement	Main performance review

Figure 2.4   Stages of performance management

PERFORMANCE MANAGEMENT ACTIVITIES

The main activities are:

▐ *Role definition,* in which the key result areas and competence requirements are agreed.

▐ *The performance agreement,* which defines expectations – what individuals have to achieve in the form of objectives, how performance will be measured and the competences needed to deliver the required results.

▌ *The performance improvement plan*, which spells out what individuals should do to improve their performance when this is necessary.

▌ *The personal development plan*, which sets out the actions people should take to develop their knowledge and skills and increase their levels of competence.

▌ *Managing performance throughout the year*, when action is taken to implement the performance agreement and performance improvement and personal development plans as individuals carry on with their day-to-day work and their planned learning activities. It includes a continuous process of providing feedback on performance, conducting informal progress reviews, updated objectives and, where necessary, dealing with performance problems.

▌ *Performance review*, which is the formal evaluation stage when a review of performance over a period takes place covering achievements, progress and problems as the basis for the next part of the continuous cycle – a revised performance agreement and performance improvement and personal development plans. It can also lead to performance ratings.

These activities are described in detail in later chapters of this book.

PERFORMANCE MANAGEMENT IN ACTION

Performance management should not be treated as a mechanistic system based on periodical formal appraisals and detailed documentation. The activities described above should be coherent in the sense of contributing to an overall systematic approach in which all aspects of the performance management process are aligned. Thus there needs to be a declaration of intent, which states why performance management is important, how it works and how people will be affected by it. The declaration should have the visible and continuous support of top management and should emphasize that the aim is to develop a high-performance culture and integrate organizational and individual goals. When developing and operating performance management it is necessary to ensure that it is regarded by all concerned as a joined-up process in which performance and development planning recorded in a performance agreement leads to continuous monitoring of performance against plans with built-in feedback. This in turn forms the basis of formal and informal reviews as and when appropriate (not just an annual event), which inform forward planning as part of a renewed performance agreement. Examples of how such an approach is made are given below.

Halifax Bank of Scotland Retail

As described by Julie Hill, HR Partner, Retail Sales, Retail Development and HEA Central Sites, HBOS, the following approach is adopted by HBOS Retail.

The essence of performance management

The essence of the HBOS Retail approach to performance management is that it is concerned with looking at how people perform not only against the requirements of the role, but also in the way they do it. The aim is to get people who are good on people skills as well as deliverables. The system has been put together to move away from ticking boxes and make it more of a reasonable and meaningful conversation as to where people are doing well and where they are doing less well.

Aim

The aim is to improve performance. Rather than just saying that somebody's been very effective and ticking a box, the process is actually to sit down and have a discussion around the requirements of the role, dealing with what aspects are being done well and what aspects are not so good. Overall the purpose is to make it clear to people how their performance links in with the performance of the business.

Achieving the aim

Performance management works very well with managers who are competent. The managers who are not so strong on the people skills are the ones who typically struggle. This is because it means that they actually have to sit down and make some judgements and discuss how they have come to their conclusions. Previously, they relied on the tick box with the answers given to them. They did not have to discuss performance. So quite a lot of coaching *has* to be done with managers for them to feel comfortable with it because the safety net of the tick box has been removed.

Principles

As described in the 'toolkit' for managers, the overriding principle is to free managers from unproductive activity and ensure that they can focus on what really matters by 'making the management of performance an organic part of everyday life, not a series of mechanical tasks and processes'. The toolkit aims to help managers manage performance:

to ensure we have a consistent approach and help us to focus on our goal of extraordinary growth by:

▌ having a simple process which removes unnecessary paperwork

▌ establishing simple, clear performance plans

▌ providing managers with a framework for recognising and differentiating colleagues' individual contribution and rewarding them through devolved pay

▌ ensuring that any issues around performance shortfalls or capability are resolved

▌ adopting the principle of 'documentation by exception'.

The key phrase is 'unleashing the performance of our people' and this is explained as follows:

Managing performance is about coaching, guiding, appraising, motivating and rewarding colleagues to help unleash potential and improve organisational performance. Where it works well it is built on excellent leadership and high quality coaching relationships between managers and teams. Through all this our colleagues should be able to answer three straightforward questions:

1. What is expected of me? How will I be clear about what is expected of me in terms of both results and behaviour?

2. How am I doing? What ongoing coaching and feedback will I receive to tell me how I am doing and how I can improve?

3. What does it mean for me? How will my individual contribution, potential and aspirations be recognised and rewarded?

Describing the role and agreeing individual expectations

Why: So colleagues have a clear picture of what is expected of them and how to achieve it.

When: Around the start of the year and reviewed to reflect organizational and individual changes, eg business objectives, role changes, development needs.

How: Discussion between the individual and line manager to agree expectations across the full range of the job (ie business performance and personal style).

What: Identify the expectations of the role using role profiles, individual job descriptions, local business objectives:

- consider the individual's performance in relation to this;
- identify / agree areas for improvement;
- documented by individual and confirmed with line manager;
- discuss how the performance requirements will be delivered, supported and reviewed.

Managing performance through coaching, observation and feedback

Why: To help individuals maximize their full contribution and potential.

When: On an ongoing basis through informal discussions, using formal review sessions only as / when required.

How: Part of everyday life through analysis of own performance:

- supported by observations, coaching and feedback from line manager and colleagues;
- not paper driven – emphasis on continuous dialogue between manager and individual concerning performance and then acting on this;
- documented by line manager by exception.

What: Recognizes performance and provides an appropriate response.

Discussing career and development opportunities

Why: To recognize individual potential and aspirations.

When: Ongoing throughout year and as a minimum once a year formal discussion.

How: A discussion between an individual and line manager to agree potential and aspirations.

For most people the process will be relatively informal and development plans will be integrated within overall development plans.

Where appropriate a more formal process reviewing potential and career aspirations will be documented through a Personal Development Review.

What: Recognizes the differing needs of those individuals with career aspirations and those who will develop in their current role.

Provides opportunity to discuss both vertical and lateral progression.

Performance matrix

A performance matrix is used for management appraisals to illustrate their performance against peers. It is not an 'appraisal rating' – the purpose of the matrix is to help individuals focus on what they do well and also any areas for improvement.

Two dimensions – business performance and behaviour (management style) are reviewed on the matrix (see Figure 2.5) to ensure a rounder discussion of overall contribution against the full role demands rather than a short-term focus on current results.

This is achieved by visual means – the individual is placed at the relevant position in the matrix by reference to the two dimensions. For example, a strong people manager who is low on the deliverables would be placed somewhere in the top left-hand quadrant but the aim will be movement to a position in the top right-hand quadrant.

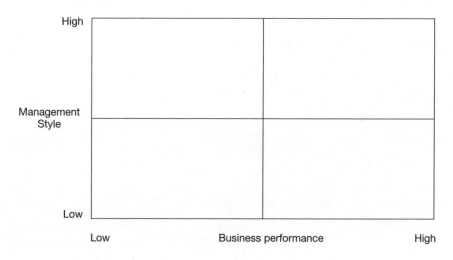

Figure 2.5   HBOS retail performance matrix

Pfizer Inc

At Pfizer Inc the guidance given on performance management is 'have a dialogue and document it'. Figure 2.6 shows how the performance management process is modelled.

Figure 2.6   Pfizer Inc performance management process

Raytheon Inc

Raytheon is a US-based defence and aerospace supplier with 80,000 employees worldwide. Its performance development process as set out by the company is modelled in Figure 2.7 and described below.

Figure 2.7   The Raytheon performance development process

Performance development

Individual and team success drive our success as a company and help us achieve our vision, to be the most admired defence and aerospace systems supplier through world-class people and technology. The Performance Development process guides the alignment of goals throughout the organization, and facilitates the achievement of meaningful objectives and the ongoing feedback needed to improve performance at every level.

Performance dialogue

One key to the success of the Performance Development process is a continuous performance dialogue. Simply stated, performance dialogue refers to the frequent and open interaction between an employee and his or her leader that begins with mutual goal setting and continues with the recognition of accomplishment, the reinforcement of desired behaviours and the identification of performance areas that can be improved. A continuous performance dialogue reflects the ongoing nature of Performance Development and supports the important elements of the Performance Development process: setting goals, tracking performance, and evaluating and rewarding performance.

Setting goals

At the beginning of each year, senior business and functional leaders meet with the CEO to discuss and set goals for the coming year. The goals fall into four major categories: customer satisfaction, people, growth and productivity. They are cascaded through the organization and employees and their leaders ensure that they are setting programme, department, team and individual objectives that align with and contribute towards the achievement of corporate and business goals. The cascaded goals help leaders and employees adjust their goals, priorities and plans, but individual goal setting begins any time. While the employee may initiate the individual goal setting using the Performance Screen (part of the web-enabled system) the process reflects collaboration and discussion between the employee and his or her supervisor to ensure that goals are aligned, meaningful, challenging and measurable. Employee goals are updated as necessary to reflect changes in priorities and new opportunities.

Tracking performance

During the year leaders have many opportunities to celebrate successes, observe behaviours, solicit and receive performance feedback from others and coach for improvement in some areas. Employees, too, track their own performance, by documenting their accomplishments against goals on their performance screen. Tracking performance, like the other performance development activities, is an ongoing process and not a once-a-year event.

Evaluating and rewarding performance

While evaluation of performance takes place every day, individual performance is summarized at least annually during the performance review discussion and documented in the Performance and Development Summary. This records the leader's assessments of strengths and areas for improvement. It also offers a place to plan training and development activities that are consistent with improving performance and supporting career development plans. The performance descriptor is one tool (of many) that helps employees understand their overall contribution and helps leaders implement Raytheon's 'pay for performance' philosophy fairly.

There is an important link between performance and rewards at all levels. Raytheon's compensation system, which is designed to offer pay that is competitive and reflective of performance, includes tools to reward at the company, programme, team and individual levels. Just as Raytheon's excellent performance on a contract may be rewarded with a contract extension, leading to increased sales, profit and continued growth, the employee's outstanding performance may lead to career progression and financial reward, recognition and personal growth. Our success is ultimately performance based and to stay competitive we need to keep improving, taking advantage of available tools and training, seeking out opportunities for feedback, and then acting on what we learn.

Scottish Parliament

The approach to performance management adopted by the Scottish Parliament as set out in the guidance notes is summarized below.

Purpose

To support the Scottish Parliament in fulfilling its constitutional role as a representative and legislative body by providing professional advice and services of the highest standards.

Aim

To be an organization in which we all behave corporately and are properly trained, informed, involved, motivated and rewarded and to which we are proud to belong.

Achieving purpose, aims and values

To help achieve the above a performance management system has been developed specifically to:

▌ Be simple to operate.

▌ Establish a clear link between business and individual objectives.

▌ Ensure commitment to our values and culture.

▌ Ensure that skills and knowledge and behaviour (competencies) are reviewed.

▌ Generate a thorough and continuing review of training and development needs.

▌ Enable us to continue to improve the organization's performance.

▌ Ensure we can identify and reward exceptional performance and contribution.

▌ Identify good and bad performance clearly.

Aims of performance management

Performance management is designed to:

▌ Ensure that what we do is guided by our values and is relevant to the purposes of the organisation.

▌ Ensure that we are all clear how to demonstrate the skills, knowledge and behaviours that are expected of us.

▌ Ensure that we are clear what our individual role is and how we intend to fulfil it.

▌ Link our job roles and individual objectives to the organisational objectives and priorities set out in the Management Plan.

▌ Ensure that all managers agree and review objectives, priorities and developmental needs with team members.

▌ Review performance against objectives and areas of competence to ensure that we are making the best possible contribution to the organisation's overall aim.

▌ Ensure that all team members receive constructive feedback in order to develop and improve performance.

▌ Ensure that a thorough review of training and development takes place as an integral part of the system so that personal development plans reflect both business and individual aims.

▌ Ensure that poor performance is identified quickly and support provided to eliminate it.

Basis of performance management

▌ Performance management involves measuring not only *whether* jobs are done but *how* they are done.

▌ Staff are assessed against a set of eight core areas of competence: 1) high-quality service, 2) flexibility and adaptability, 3) personal contribution, 4) problem solving and decision making, 5) leadership/teamwork, 6) communication and interpersonal skills, 7) parliamentary awareness and 8) equal opportunities – improving access and promoting equality. The competency areas are aligned to the job evaluation scheme factors.

▌ Positive and negative indicators exist against each area of competence to illustrate the ways in which staff are expected to behave and the ways in which they are expected not to behave.

Good performance management

Good performance management is achieved through both parties ensuring that:

▌ New staff know what is expected of them from the outset.

▌ Everyone is clear about corporate goals and works towards them.

▌ Objectives are SMART (Specific, Measurable, Achievable, Relevant, Time related).

▌ A system exists to accommodate day-to-day performance feedback.

▌ The personal development plan (PDP) is used formally to help self-developmental activities and/or improve performance.

▮ The line manager provides and the jobholder undertakes the training needed to support the individual and the organization.

▮ Appropriate support is in place to eliminate poor performance.

Personal development plan

A personal development plan is an important part of the system. It is a plan on which to record:

▮ where the level of competence is met but where we would like to develop further;

▮ any training and/or development needed to support the delivery of that objective;

▮ any gaps in skills, knowledge or behaviours that need to be overcome in order to meet our objectives.

It gives jobholders and line managers the opportunity to:

▮ identify, discuss and agree development needs for the year ahead;

▮ prioritize and plan how these will be addressed and achieved;

▮ agree and set dates for reviewing the plan;

▮ if necessary, plan how poor performance might be improved.

Standard Chartered Bank

The approach to performance management as described by Caroline Sharley, Organization Development Manager, is described below.

Background

Standard Chartered Bank is a global business engaged in retail and wholesale banking, which is based in Hong Kong and has about 30,000 employees.

Features and aims of performance management

▮ Annual cycle – objective setting in January, interim review in July and final review in November/December (see Figure 2.8).

▮ Set a climate in which high management performance is seen to be important (see Figure 2.9).

▌ The emphasis is on 'managing for excellence – help people understand what excellence means and how they can achieve it'.

▌ Set objectives that play to people's strengths.

▌ First crucial question: 'How do we get people to do their best every day within the objectives they are set?'

▌ Second crucial question: 'How can we get people to go from good to great?'

▌ 'Performance management is all about behaviour.'

▌ 'Each year there has to be a build-up of stretch in objectives.'

▌ 'What was excellent last year is doing your job this year.'

▌ Set three types of objectives: financial/business objectives, two core management objectives and a values objective for all.

Getting performance management to work

▌ 'Put into place the enablers that will make it happen.'

▌ Total commitment from senior management. Much time spent in engaging line managers in the process. Performance management a regular topic at senior management meetings.

▌ Central focus on training – skills workshops.

▌ Use Gallup Poll survey to measure engagement.

Rating

Two scales:

1. Financial, achieving business objectives, 1 to 5 scale.

2. 'Living the values', four-point (A to D) scale – aim is 'to drive changes in behaviour'.

The objective is to get ratings across the whole of the scales and encourage managers to adopt a more courageous approach.

If a business is delivering its objectives it would be expected to have a normal distribution of ratings.

If a business is delivering at a high level, the distribution would be expected to be skewed positively.

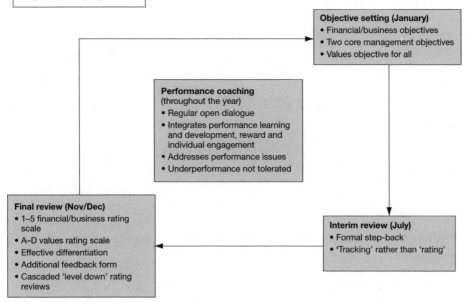

Figure 2.8 Standard Chartered Bank: managing for high performance

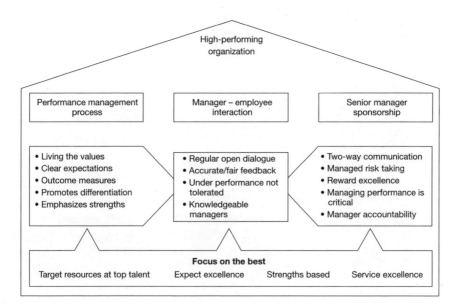

Figure 2.9 Standard Chartered Bank: managing for high performance – the future

Models of performance management

Models of the performance management processes used in three organizations are set out in Figures 2.10, 2.11 and 2.12.

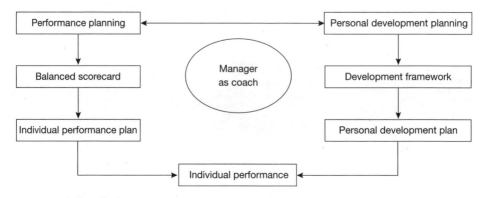

Figure 2.10 Performance management in a building society

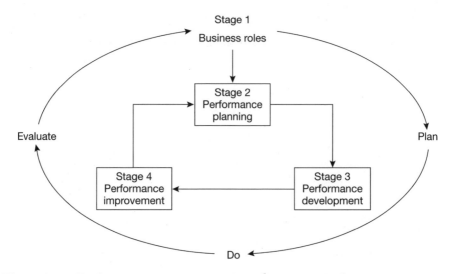

Figure 2.11 Performance management in a pharmaceutical company

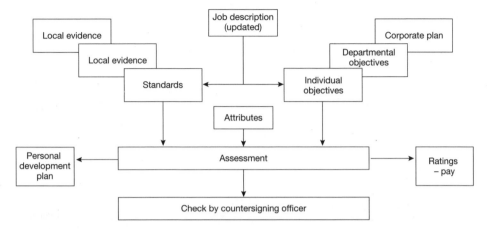

Figure 2.12   Performance management in a not-for-profit organization

REFERENCE

1   Deming, W E (1986) *Out of the Crisis*, MIT Centre for Advanced Engineering Study, Cambridge, MA

3

The practice of performance management

A considerable amount of research has been carried out recently on how organizations put performance management into effect by IRS (1), Ed Lawler and Michael McDermott (2), the CIPD (3) and e-reward (4). In this chapter the findings of these research projects are summarized and conclusions drawn from them on current performance management practices.

IRS, 2003

The IRS survey in 2003 covered 47 organizations. It established that there were three main approaches to performance management:

1. *A clear strategy* – a systematic approach with a formal policy aligning all aspects of the performance management process. Just under half of the respondents (48 per cent) adopted this approach.

2. *A general approach* – policies exist in areas such as employee development, appraisal, and job evaluation, but there was no overall performance management strategy. This approach was adopted by 42 per cent of the respondents.

3. *A few initiatives* – an ad hoc approach existed to performance management, with policies in some areas but not others and little coordination overall. This approach was adopted by 10 per cent of the respondents.

The survey respondents were also asked about the extent to which they had a performance culture in their organizations and 30 per cent said 'a lot', 53 per cent said 'a fair amount' and 17 per cent said 'a little'.

Finally, respondents were asked to assess the effectiveness of their performance management practices. The practices that had 'a lot of effect' on performance as indicated by the percentage of respondents who believed this to be the case were:

▌ on-the-job training – 81 per cent;

▌ employee appraisals – 77 per cent;

▌ performance-related bonus – 44 per cent;

▌ cascading information via managers – 54 per cent;

▌ competence frameworks – 54 per cent;

▌ business strategy of continuous improvement – 50 per cent.

The significance of on-the-job-training and performance appraisals is noteworthy. It is also interesting to note that, as IRS put it, 'despite the hype about the new technology', only 13 per cent of respondents felt that e-learning had made a lot of difference to performance. Individual performance pay also did quite badly, with only 35 per cent believing that it had made a lot of difference.

LAWLER AND MCDERMOTT, 2003

Ed Lawler and Michael McDermott surveyed 55 HR managers from large and medium-sized United States organizations with questions about the nature of their performance management systems and their effectiveness. In 86 per cent of the organizations there were consistent and company-wide performance management practices. The main findings were as follows:

▌ Business strategy-driven performance goals and jointly set individual goals, which formed parts of the approach adopted by the majority of organizations, make a positive contribution to performance management.

▌ Ongoing feedback by managers is strongly related to performance management effectiveness. As stated by the researchers: 'The results strongly suggest that organizations should build ongoing feedback into their systems.'

▌ There was a particularly strong relationship between effectiveness and using measures of how individuals accomplish their results. The comment made by the researchers was that: 'This strongly suggests that systems work when people are appraised on both their results and how they obtain them.'

▌ The results of the survey also suggested that using competencies and developmental planning makes a significant impact in terms of creating an effective performance management system.

▌ Effectiveness is higher when rewards are tied to appraisals.

▌ 360-degree appraisal was not widely used and was not likely to be used for financial reward purposes.

▌ If the performance management system is going to be tied into business strategy, it is critical that senior management make that tie.

▌ It is important that line managers own the performance management system.

▌ The correlation between the presence of training and the effectiveness of performance appraisals was very high.

▌ Web-enabled (e-HR) systems were used in 57 per cent of the organization (this contrasts with the mere 16 per cent of UK organizations using such systems as established by the 2005 e-reward survey).

▌ Individual performance management practices need to be driven by the business strategy and fit with one another and with the overall human resource management system of the organization.

CHARTERED INSTITUTE OF PERSONNEL AND DEVELOPMENT, 2003

The CIPD survey of performance management in December 2003 covered 506 respondents. The key data emerging from the survey were as follows:

▌ 87 per cent operated a formal performance management process (36 per cent of these were new systems).

▌ 71 per cent agreed that the focus of performance management is developmental.

▌ 62 per cent used objective setting.

▌ 31 per cent used competence assessment.

▌ 14 per cent used 360-degree feedback.

▌ 62 per cent used personal development plans.

▌ 59 per cent gave an overall rating for performance; 40 per cent did not.

▌ The number of rating levels used:
  – 3: 6 per cent;
  – 4: 28 per cent;
  – 5: 47 per cent;
  – 6+: 17 per cent.

▌ 8 per cent used forced distribution to guide ratings.

▌ 55 per cent disagreed that pay contingent on performance is an essential part of performance management.

▌ 42 per cent used ratings to inform contingent pay decisions; 52 per cent did not.

▌ 31 per cent had performance-related pay.

▌ 7 per cent had competence-related pay.

▌ 4 per cent had contribution-related pay.

▌ 3 per cent had team pay.

▌ 46 per cent separate performance management reviews from pay reviews; 26 per cent did not.

▌ 75 per cent agreed that performance management motivates individuals; 22 per cent disagreed.

▌ 80 per cent agreed that line managers own and operate the performance management process; 20 per cent disagreed.

▌ The extent to which buy-in to performance management is obtained from line managers is:
  – completely and actively in favour: 15 per cent;
  – most generally accept that it is useful: 62 per cent;

- most are indifferent but go through the motions: 22 per cent;
- most are hostile: 1 per cent.

▌ 61 per cent of line managers believe that performance management is very or mostly effective; 37 per cent believe it is partly effective or ineffective.

▌ 37 per cent of other staff believe that performance management is very or mostly effective; 58 per cent believe it is partly effective or ineffective.

▌ 71 per cent agreed that the focus of performance management is developmental; 27 per cent disagreed.

▌ 42 per cent agreed that pay contingent on performance is an essential part of performance management; 55 per cent disagreed.

▌ 42 per cent of respondents agreed that performance management should be distanced as far as possible from payment systems; 56 per cent disagreed.

E-REWARD, 2005

The outcomes of the e-reward survey of performance management held in April 2005 covering 181 respondents are summarized below.

Incidence of performance management

▌ 96 per cent had performance management.

▌ Over half had operated performance management for more than five years.

▌ In 91 per cent of respondents' organizations, performance management covered all jobs.

Principal features of performance management processes

▌ Almost all respondents used objective setting and performance review.

▌ Personal development plans were used in 89 per cent of organizations and performance improvement plans in 74 per cent.

▌ 24 per cent of respondents reported that they were using or developing competence frameworks as part of the process.

▌ 30 per cent used 360-degree feedback.

Objectives of performance management

The six top objectives of performance management were:

▮ to align individual and organizational objectives – 64 per cent;

▮ to improve organizational performance – 63 per cent;

▮ to improve individual performance – 46 per cent;

▮ to provide the basis for personal development – 37 per cent;

▮ to develop a performance culture – 32 per cent;

▮ to inform contribution/performance pay decisions – 21 per cent.

It is interesting to note that informing contribution/performance pay decisions comes a poor sixth in the list.

The following is a typical statement of objectives from one respondent: 'Supporting culture change by creating a performance culture and reinforcing the values of the organization with an emphasis on the importance of these in getting a balance between "what" is delivered and "how" it is delivered.'

Changes to performance management

Seventy-four per cent of the organizations had made major changes to their processes over the last five years and 47 per cent proposed to make further changes in the next 12 months.

The main changes made over the last five years were:

▮ introducing competence analysis – 23;

▮ abandoning competence analysis – 3;

▮ performance agreements – 18;

▮ enhance link to pay – 17;

▮ performance reviews – 15;

▮ achieving consistency – 14;

▮ one set of performance management processes – 13;

▮ alignment of corporate strategy and objectives – 13;

▮ simplification – 11;

▮ rating – 9;

▌ introduce web-based approaches – 8;

▌ 360-degree feedback – 5;

▌ personal development – 5.

The planned changes mentioned by respondents were:

▌ enhance link to pay – 16;

▌ achieve more consistency – 10;

▌ introduce competence analysis – 9;

▌ introduce web-based systems – 8;

▌ review rating processes – 8;

▌ simplify – 6;

▌ introduce one system of performance management for all – 5;

▌ introduce 360-degree feedback – 4.

The fact that interest in contribution or performance pay continues is interesting.

Contingent pay and rating

The following types of contingent pay were used by respondents:

▌ individual performance-related pay – 57 per cent;

▌ contribution-related pay – 30 per cent;

▌ service-related pay – 20 per cent;

▌ competence-related pay – 17 per cent.

The median increase given in 2004 was 3 per cent.

Fifty-nine per cent of those with contribution or performance pay used overall ratings as the basis for determining increases but 23 per cent had overall ratings that were *not* linked to performance or contribution pay.

The methods used to determine and control increases were:

▌ pay matrix – 45 per cent;

▌ guidelines – 32 per cent;

▌ forced choice distribution – 12 per cent.

Overall ratings were used by 70 per cent of respondents. The most popular number of levels was five (43 per cent of respondents).

Training

Formal training for line managers was provided by 86 per cent of respondents, 45 per cent used coaching and 46 per cent of respondents offer formal training to both line managers and staff.

Web-based methods of administering performance management

A relatively small number of respondents (16 per cent) used web-based methods of administering performance management.

Performance management issues

Concern was expressed by respondents about the following issues:

▮ Line managers do not have the skills required – 88 per cent.

▮ Line managers do not discriminate sufficiently when assessing performance – 84 per cent.

▮ Line managers are not committed to performance management – 75 per cent.

▮ Line managers are reluctant to conduct performance management reviews – 74 per cent.

▮ 49 per cent believed that staff were more demotivated than motivated by performance management: a sad reflection on its effectiveness.

▮ 44 per cent believed that the link between performance management and pay was inappropriate.

▮ 40 per cent believed that there was no evidence that performance management improved performance.

Dealing with the issues

More training or coaching for managers was the most popular method of dealing with the issues. A number of respondents were reviewing the process and some were seeking greater support from top management. Here are some typical comments:

'There is a shift in culture from long-term employees feeling that performance management is just something they have to go through, but that they will be in the job for ever anyway, to a more businesslike approach to performance management, with accountability, and competency.'

'Structured programme of line management training is being established with great success. Ongoing coaching of those managers is taking place.'

'Line managers tend to give the average 3c rating, and back away from dealing with poor performance. We conduct regular coaching sessions with line managers to encourage them to actively performance-manage.'

'After introducing a new scheme three years ago, last year we carried out a refresher training workshop specifically tackling how to carry out performance reviews, feedback and dealing with poor performance. The majority of managers found this useful, but there remains a significant number who believe that the training was unnecessary.'

'Generating leadership from the top of the hierarchy to support/ encourage the need for managers to tackle poor performance head on in a fair and positive manner.'

'We are seeking ways of getting the executive team to take ownership of our performance management system and to get the buy-in of their management teams to work with it for the benefit of the organization. Alongside this, we are asking them to encourage their management teams to participate in relevant development to improve their skills so that they may be more effective.'

'We are currently reviewing the organization's performance management processes, with a view to implementing a revised system to aid and support the process. We are also looking for performance management to shift from the twice-yearly appraisal and become more obviously integrated in day-to-day management.'

'Nagging, nagging, nagging, motivating, threatening, nagging etc.'

Impact of performance management

- Very significant – 32 per cent.
- Fairly significant – 36 per cent.
- Insignificant – 10 per cent.
- Not known – 22 per cent.

Implications

The most significant implications of the survey as discussed below are derived from the eminently practical and realistic comments from respondents on what makes performance management work.

Achieving buy-in from top management

A constantly recurring plea in every area of HR policy is that there must be active support from top management if it is to be effective. This is particularly the case with performance management as it is up to them to impress on everyone in the organization that the achievement of high levels of performance is a fundamental part of the organization's method of operation and that performance management is regarded as a major instrument in developing and maintaining a performance culture. Clearly, this means that they must engage wholeheartedly in performance management processes themselves as an integral part of how they approach their role as managers. But they have also to deliver and reiterate the message that they expect all line managers to do the same. In other words, it is top management, and only top management, that can ensure that performance management becomes a key part of the culture of the organization – 'the way we do things around here'.

It could be argued that without that support – in deeds as well as words – there is no real point in pursuing performance management. In some cases, the support is readily available; in others, HR as a business partner has a key role to play in enlisting and perpetuating it. A business case has to be made for performance management, which means it has to be presented as a business process (a business improvement model), not an HR activity. HR is concerned because performance management is about the management and development of people and it is the role of HR to manage communications about performance management on behalf of top management, to ensure the involvement of staff in its development and to provide the training, coaching and guidance that are essential to its success. Ultimately, however, performance management has to be seen and presented by top management as a means of helping them to run the business.

Achieving line management commitment and capability

The comments from respondents about the issues surrounding performance management confirmed that, given top management support, its effectiveness depended largely on the commitment of line managers to the processes and the level of skill they could bring to bear in carrying them out. It is line managers who 'do' performance management. If they do it badly it will fail.

Explanations of why the alarming figure of 49 per cent of respondents reported that performance management demotivated rather than motivated staff were not available (this could well be the subject of further research), but it is a reasonable assumption that the unwillingness or inability of line managers to do it properly were major causes of the problem. Perfunctory reviews, inadequate or biased feedback, a judgemental approach and unwillingness to engage in dialogue can all demotivate people.

But this should not be regarded as a blanket criticism of line managers. It is up to HR to ensure through communication, involvement and, above all, training and coaching that they believe in what they have to do, willingly find time to do it, and have the skills to do it well. And these skills such as agreeing objectives, using competency frameworks, providing feedback, coaching, and discussing improvement and development plans are demanding. This is not a problem that can be solved by the issue of a glossy brochure and a half-day training course. It needs continuous and sometimes frustrating effort. Complete success will never be achieved. There will always be some line managers who are not up to it. If they still exist, having been given training, coaching and guidance, and leadership from the top, then their fitness as people managers must be questioned.

Clarity in purpose and process and simplicity in operation

Again and again respondents emphasized the need to be clear about the objectives of performance management and about the processes to be used. The whole system must be transparent – everyone should know how it works, how it affects them and how the outcomes of performance management will be used. Above all, the message delivered by respondents was 'keep it simple'. Elaborate forms, lots of paperwork and bureaucratic procedures are the death of performance management and provide the best way of putting everyone concerned off the process.

Alignment and integration

As a business improvement model, performance management must ensure that individual objectives are aligned to organizational objectives and any discrepancies in performance need to be dealt with through improvement and personal development plans. Performance management should not be regarded as a stand-alone process; it needs to be treated as part of the normal way of doing business, which is linked strongly to other HR activities, especially those concerned with learning and development.

Cultural fit

Performance management processes must fit the culture of the organization – the way it 'does the business', and its values and norms. As a number of respondents commented, the system should never be 'lifted down from the shelf' and if management consultants are used they should demonstrate that they understand the culture and are presenting recommendations that are aligned to that culture.

Contribution and performance pay

There was a strong tendency for respondents to question too much focus on financial reward as an outcome of performance management. Of course, if people are going to be rewarded according to their contribution or performance then some attempt has got to be made to assess that contribution or performance. But the danger of creating a formulaic link between a performance appraisal rating and a pay increase is that performance management is regarded simply as a means of creating a link rather than as an approach to performance improvement and development.

The care and time factors

Respondents frequently mentioned the need to take great care in planning performance management – obtaining the views of stakeholders, pilot testing, considering all the implications, obtaining buy-in and commitment. The overall message was that developing performance management 'takes longer than you think' and some respondents commented that it is best not to be too ambitious to start with. It was also remarked by several respondents that time has to be allowed to embed performance management. It won't happen overnight. People have got to be given time to get used to the idea and develop the attitudes and skills required for it to work.

Evaluation

It is hard to see how performance management can be improved as it is progressively embedded without evaluating its effectiveness. Yet less than half of respondents did evaluate. It is essential to find out how well it is operating so that communication, training, coaching and guidance can be provided where necessary. But several respondents warned against tinkering too much with the basic processes on the grounds that this only serves to confuse people.

Conclusion

The overall implication of this survey is that performance management is by no means an easy option. It should never be entered into lightly and without taking account of and acting on the implications set out above.

REFERENCES

1 IRS Employment Review (2003) Performance management: policy and practice, August, pp 12–19
2 Lawler, E E and McDermott, M (2003) Current performance management practices, *WorldatWork Journal*, Second quarter, pp 49–60
3 Armstrong, M and Baron, A (2004) *Managing Performance: Performance management in action*, CIPD, London
4 e-reward (2005) *Survey of Performance Management Practice*, e-reward, Stockport

4

Performance planning and agreements

PERFORMANCE AND DEVELOPMENT PLANNING

Performance management helps people to get into action so that they achieve planned and agreed results. It focuses on what has to be done, how it should be done and what is to be achieved. But it is equally concerned with developing people – helping them to learn – and providing them with the support they need to do well, now and in the future. The framework for performance management is provided by the performance agreement, which is the outcome of performance and development planning. The agreement provides the basis for managing performance throughout the year and for guiding improvement and development activities. It is used as a reference point when reviewing performance and the achievement of improvement and development plans.

Performance and development planning is carried out jointly by the manager and the individual. These discussions should lead to an agreement on what needs to be done by both parties. The starting point for the performance and development plans is provided by the role profile, which defines the results, knowledge and skills and behaviours required. This provides the basis for agreeing objectives and performance measures. Performance and personal development plans are derived from an analysis of role requirements and performance in meeting them. These areas are covered in this chapter under the headings:

- role profiles;

- objective setting;

- performance measures and assessment;

- performance planning;

- development planning;

- the performance agreement.

ROLE PROFILES

The basis of the performance and development agreement is a role profile, which defines the role in terms of the key results expected, what role holders are expected to know and be able to do (technical competencies), and how they are expected to behave in terms of behavioural competencies and upholding the organization's core values. Role profiles need to be updated every time a formal performance agreement is developed. An example of a role profile is shown in Figure 4.1.

Developing role profiles

To develop a role profile it is necessary for the line manager and the individual to get together and agree key result areas, define what the role holder needs to know and be able to do and ensure that there is mutual understanding of the behavioural competencies required and the core values the role holder is expected to uphold.

Defining key result areas

When introducing performance management it is probably best to abandon any existing job descriptions. They may well be out of date and probably go into far too much detail about what is to be done rather than focusing on what has to be achieved.

Role title: Database administrator

Department: Information systems

Purpose of role: Responsible for the development and support of databases and their underlying environment.

Key result areas:

▌ Identify database requirements for all projects that require data management in order to meet the needs of internal customers.

▌ Develop project plans collaboratively with colleagues to deliver against their database needs.

▌ Support underlying database infrastructure.

▌ Liaise with system and software providers to obtain product information and support.

▌ Manage project resources (people and equipment) within predefined budget and criteria, as agreed with line manager and originating department.

▌ Allocate work to and supervise contractors on day-to-day basis.

▌ Ensure security of the underlying database infrastructure through adherence to established protocols and to develop additional security protocols where needed.

Need to know:

▌ Oracle database administration.

▌ Operation of Designer 2000 and Oracle forms SQL/PLSQL, Unix administration, shell programming.

Able to:

▌ Analyse and choose between options where the solution is not always obvious.

▌ Develop project plans and organize own workload on a timescale of 1-2 months.

▌ Adapt to rapidly changing needs and priorities without losing sight of overall plans and priorities.

▌ Interpret budgets in order to manage resources effectively within them.

▌ Negotiate with suppliers.

▌ Keep abreast of technical developments and trends, bring these into day-to-day work when feasible and build them into new project developments.

Behavioural competencies:

▌ Aim to get things done well and set and meet challenging goals, create own measures of excellence and constantly seek ways of improving performance.

▌ Analyse information from range of sources and develop effective solutions/ recommendations.

▌ Communicate clearly and persuasively, orally or in writing, dealing with technical issues in a non-technical manner.

▌ Work participatively on projects with technical and non-technical colleagues.

▌ Develop positive relationships with colleagues as the supplier of an internal service.

Figure 4.1 A role profile

To define key result areas individuals should be asked by their manager to answer questions such as:

▌ What do you think are the most important things you have to do?

▌ What do you believe you are expected to achieve in each of these areas?

▌ How will you – or anyone else – know whether or not you have achieved them?

The answers to these questions may need to be sorted out – they can often result in a mass of jumbled information that has to be analysed so that the various activities can be distinguished and refined to seven or eight key areas. This process requires some skill, which needs to be developed by training followed by practice. It is an area in which HR specialists can usefully coach and follow up on a one-to-one basis after an initial training session.

Defining technical competencies

To define technical competencies, ie what people need to know and be able to do, three questions need to be answered:

▌ To perform this role effectively, what has the role holder to be able to do with regard to each of the key result areas?

▌ What knowledge and skills in terms of qualifications, technical and procedural knowledge, problem-solving, planning and communication skills etc do role holders need to carry out the role effectively?

▌ How will anyone know when the role has been carried out well?

Defining behavioural competencies

The usual approach to including behavioural competencies in the performance agreement is to use a competency framework developed for the organization. The manager and the individual can then discuss the implications of the framework at the planning stage. The following is an example of a competence framework:

▌ *Personal drive* – demonstrate the drive to achieve, acting confidently with decisiveness and resilience.

▌ *Business awareness* – identify and explore business opportunities, understand the business concerns and priorities of the organization and constantly seek methods of ensuring that the organization becomes more businesslike.

▌ *Teamwork* – work cooperatively and flexibly with other members of the team with a full understanding of the role to be played as a team member.

▌ *Communication* – communicate clearly and persuasively, orally or in writing.

▌ *Customer focus* – exercise unceasing care in looking after the interests of external and internal customers to ensure that their wants, needs and expectations are met or exceeded.

▌ *Developing others* – foster the development of members of his or her team, providing feedback, support, encouragement and coaching.

▌ *Flexibility* – adapt to and work effectively in different situations and carry out a variety of tasks.

▌ *Leadership* – guide, encourage and motivate individuals and teams to achieve a desired result.

▌ *Planning* – decide on courses of action, ensuring that the resources required to implement the action will be available and scheduling the programme of work required to achieve a defined end-result.

▌ *Problem solving* – analyse situations, diagnose problems, identify the key issues, establish and evaluate alternative courses of action and produce a logical, practical and acceptable solution.

Core values

Increasingly, performance management is being used by organizations to encourage people 'to live the values'. These values can include such concerns as quality, continuous improvement, customer service, innovation, care and consideration for people, environmental issues and equal opportunity. Discussions held when the performance agreement is being reached can define what these values mean as far as individual behaviour is concerned.

The Scottish Parliament emphasizes that assessing how well people uphold core values is an integral part of performance management, stating that:

Our success depends on all of us sharing the common values set out in the management plan, ie:

Integrity	We demonstrate high standards of honesty and reliability.
Impartiality	We are fair and even-handed in dealing with members of the public and each other.
Professionalism	We provide high quality professional advice and support services.
Client focus	We are responsive to the needs of members, the public and one another.
Efficiency	We use resources responsibly and cost-effectively.
Mutual respect	We treat everyone with respect and courtesy and take full account of equal opportunities issues at all times.

OBJECTIVE SETTING

Objectives describe something that has to be accomplished. Objectives or goals (the terms are interchangeable) define what organizations, functions, departments and individuals are expected to achieve over a period of time. Objective setting that results in an agreement on what the role holder has to achieve is an important part of the performance management processes of defining and managing expectations and forms the point of reference for performance reviews.

Types of objectives

The different types of objectives and how they are set are described below.

Ongoing role or work objectives

All roles have built-in objectives, which may be expressed as key result areas in a role profile. The definition of a key result area states that this is what the role holder is expected to achieve in this particular aspect of the role. For example: 'Identify database requirements for all projects that require data management in order to meet the needs of internal customers' or 'Deal quickly with customer queries in order to create and maintain high levels of satisfaction.'

A key result area statement should contain an indication of not only what has to be done but also why it has to be done. The 'why' part clarifies the ongoing objective but it may be necessary to expand that by reaching agreement on a performance standard that describes what good performance will look like. A performance standard definition should take the form of a statement that performance will be up to standard if a desirable, specified and observable result happens. It should preferably be quantified in terms, for example, of level of service or speed of response. Where this is not possible, a more qualitative approach may have to be adopted, in which case the standard of performance definition would in effect state: 'This job or task will have been well done when… (the following things happen).'

Good role or work objectives will clearly define the activity in terms of the results and standards to be achieved. They may be supplemented by quantified targets. Although described as ongoing, they need to be reviewed regularly and, as necessary, modified.

Targets

Targets are objectives that define the quantifiable results to be attained as measured in such terms as output, throughput, income, sales, levels of service delivery, cost reduction and reduction of reject rates. Thus a customer service target could be to respond to 90 per cent of queries within two working days.

Tasks/projects

Objectives can be set for the completion of tasks or projects by a specified date or to achieve an interim result. A target for a database administrator could be to develop a new database to meet the need of the HR department by the end of the year.

Behavioural expectations

Behavioural expectations are often set out generally in competency frameworks but they may also be defined individually under the framework headings. Competency frameworks may deal with areas of behaviour associated with core values, for example teamwork, but they often convert the aspirations contained in value statements into more specific examples of desirable and undesirable behaviour, which can help in planning and reviewing performance.

Values

Expectations can be defined for upholding the core values of the organization. The aim would be to ensure that espoused values become values in use.

Performance improvement

Performance improvement objectives define what needs to be done to achieve better results. They may be expressed in a performance improvement plan, which specifies what actions need to be taken by role holders *and* their managers. Approaches to performance improvement are discussed in Chapter 8.

Developmental/learning

Developmental or learning objectives specify areas for personal development and learning in the shape of enhanced knowledge and skills (abilities and competences). They will be recorded in a personal development plan as described in Chapter 10.

What is a good objective?

Good work objectives and targets are:

▌ *consistent* with the values of the organization and departmental and organizational objectives;

▌ *precise:* clear and well defined, using positive words;

▌ *challenging:* to stimulate high standards of performance and to encourage progress;

▌ *measurable:* related to quantified or qualitative performance measures;

▌ *achievable:* within the capabilities of the individual – account should be taken of any constraints that might affect the individual's capacity to achieve the objectives; these could include lack of resources (money, time, equipment, support from other people), lack of experience or training, external factors beyond the individual's control etc;

▌ *agreed* by the manager and the individual concerned – the aim is to provide for the ownership, not the imposition, of objectives, although there may be situations where individuals have to be persuaded to accept a higher standard than they believe themselves to be capable of attaining;

▌ *time related*: achievable within a defined timescale (this would not be applicable to a role or work objective);

▌ *focused on teamwork*: emphasize the need to work as an effective member of a team as well as individual achievement.

Many organizations use the following 'SMART' mnemonic to summarize the characteristics of good objectives:

S = *Specific/stretching* – clear, unambiguous, straightforward, under-standable and challenging.
M = *Measurable* – quantity, quality, time, money.
A = *Achievable* – challenging but within the reach of a competent and committed person.
R = *Relevant* – relevant to the objectives of the organization so that the goal of the individual is aligned to corporate goals.
T = *Time framed* – to be completed within an agreed timescale.

Integrating objectives

A defining characteristic of performance management is the importance attached to the integration or alignment of individual objectives with organizational objectives. The aim is to focus people on doing the right things in order to achieve a shared understanding of performance requirements throughout the organization.

The integration of organizational and individual and team objectives is often referred to as a process of 'cascading objectives'. However, cascading should not be regarded as just a top-down process. There will be overarching corporate goals, but people at each level should be given the opportunity to indicate how they believe they can contribute to the attainment of team and departmental objectives. This is a 'bottom-up' process, and the views of employees about what they believe they can achieve should be noted and, as appropriate, higher-level objectives amended to take account of them. An approach along these lines increases 'ownership' of the objectives as well as providing a channel for upward communication on key issues affecting the achievement of business goals. Of course there will be times when the overriding challenge has to be accepted, but there will also be many occasions when the opinions of those who have to do the work will be well worth listening to.

Integration is achieved by ensuring that everyone is aware of corporate, functional and team goals and that the objectives they agree for themselves are consistent with those goals and will contribute in specified ways to their achievement. This process is illustrated in Figure 4.2.

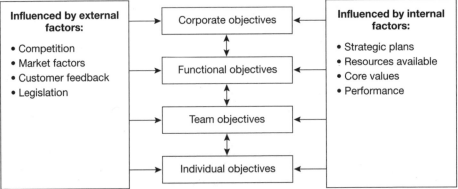

Figure 4.2   Integration of objectives

Figure 4.3 illustrates how objectives can be integrated in a specific area.

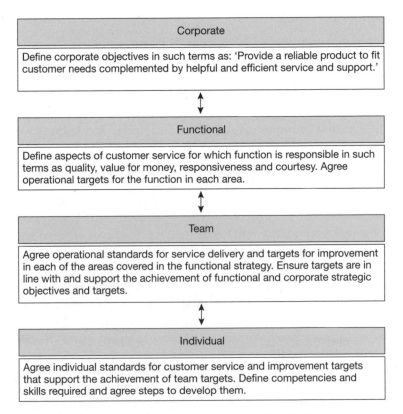

Figure 4.3   Two-way process of agreeing integrated objectives

Objective-setting checklist

1. Has the objective-setting process been based on an agreed and up-to-date role profile that sets out key result areas?

2. Has objective setting been carried out jointly with your manager?

3. Are your standards and targets clearly related to the key result areas in your role profile?

4. Do your objectives clearly and specifically support the achievement of your team and functional objectives and, ultimately, corporate objectives. If so, how?

5. Are your objectives specific?

6. Do they provide some challenge to you?

7. Are they realistic and attainable?

8. Has a time limit for their achievement been agreed?

9. How will you know that your objectives have been achieved?

10. Have any problems you may meet in attaining your objectives been identified and has action to overcome these problems been agreed?

PERFORMANCE MEASURES AND ASSESSMENT

It is often said that, 'if you can't measure it, you can't manage it' and 'what gets measured gets done'. Certainly, you cannot improve performance until you know what present performance is.

The process of managing performance begins by defining expectations in terms of targets, standards and competence requirements. But improvements to performance and personal development programmes have to start from an understanding of what the level of current performance is in terms of both results and competence. This is the basis for identifying improvement and development needs if there is a shortfall. More positively, it provides the information required for career planning and continuous development by identifying strengths to be enhanced as well as weaknesses to be overcome. But this can only be achieved if there are agreed and reliable performance measures or criteria for assessment. Performance management involves encouraging people to take charge of their own performance. This cannot be done unless they can measure, assess and therefore monitor progress towards their goals.

Measurement is an important concept in performance management. It is the basis for providing and generating feedback, it identifies where things are going well to provide the foundations for building further success, and it indicates where things are not going so well, so that corrective action can be taken. In general, it provides the basis for answering two fundamental questions: 'Is what is being done worth doing?' and 'Has it been done well?'

Measurement and assessment issues – outputs, outcomes and inputs

It can be argued that what gets measured is often what is easy to measure. And in some jobs what is meaningful is not measurable and what is measurable is not meaningful. It was asserted by Levinson (1) that: 'The greater the emphasis on measurement and quantification, the more likely the subtle, non-measurable elements of the task will be sacrificed. Quality of performance frequently, therefore, loses out to quantification.'

Measuring performance is relatively easy for those who are responsible for achieving quantified targets, for example sales. It is more difficult in the case of knowledge workers, for example scientists. But this difficulty is alleviated if a distinction is made between the two forms of results – outputs and outcomes.

Outputs and outcomes

An output is a result that can be measured quantifiably, while an outcome is a visible effect that is the result of effort but cannot necessarily be measured in quantified terms.

There are components in all jobs that are difficult to measure quantifiably as outputs. But all jobs produce outcomes even if they are not quantified. It is therefore often necessary to measure performance by reference to what outcomes have been attained in comparison with what outcomes were expected, and the outcomes may be expressed in qualitative terms as a standard or level of competence to be attained. That is why it is important when agreeing objectives to answer the question: 'How will we know that this objective has been achieved?' The answer needs to be expressed in the form: 'Because such and such will have happened.' The 'such and such' will be defined either as outputs in such forms as meeting or exceeding a quantified target or completing a project or task satisfactorily (what is 'satisfactory' having been defined), or as outcomes in such forms as reaching an agreed standard of performance or delivering an agreed level of service.

Classification of output and outcome measures

Output measures or metrics include:

▌ financial measures – income, shareholder value, added value, rates of return, costs;

▌ units produced or processed, throughput;

▌ level of take-up of a service;

▌ sales, new accounts;

▌ time measures – speed of response or turnaround, achievements compared with timetables, amount of backlog, time to market, delivery times.

Outcome measures include:

▌ attainment of a standard (quality, level of service etc);

▌ changes in behaviour;

▌ completion of work/project;

▌ acquisition and effective use of additional knowledge and skills;

▌ reaction – judgement by others, colleagues, internal and external customers.

Inputs – competency and upholding core values

However, when assessing performance it is also necessary to consider inputs in the shape of the degree of knowledge and skill attained and behaviour that is demonstrably in line with the standards set out in competency frameworks and statements of core values. It is emphasized by Risher (2) that it is important to encourage behaviours such as the following:

▌ builds effective working relationships with others;

▌ takes the initiative to address problems;

▌ seeks knowledge related to emerging issues;

▌ shares know-how and information with co-workers;

▌ responds effectively to customer concerns.

In the Scottish Parliament the competency headings used are: 1) high-quality service, 2) flexibility and adaptability, 3) personal contribution, 4) problem solving and decision making, 5) leadership/teamwork, 6) communication and interpersonal skills, 7) parliamentary awareness, 8) equal opportunities – improving access and promoting equality.

Assessing competency

Positive and negative indicators for competency headings in a framework can be devised and used as the basis for assessments in the following example for leadership.

Positive indicators

▌ Achieves high level of performance from team.

▌ Defines objectives, plans and expectations clearly.

▌ Continually monitors performance and provides good feedback.

▌ Maintains effective relationships with individuals and the team as a whole.

▌ Develops a sense of common purpose in the team.

▌ Builds team morale and effectively motivates individual members of the team by recognizing their contribution while taking appropriate action to deal with poor performers.

Negative indicators

▌ Does not achieve high levels of performance from team.

▌ Fails to clarify objectives or standards of performance.

▌ Pays insufficient attention to the needs of individuals and the team.

▌ Neither monitors nor provides effective feedback on performance.

▌ Inconsistent in rewarding good performance or taking action to deal with poor performance.

Competencies can also be set out in the form of a scale to provide a basis for assessment as in the following example for a personal drive competency:

1. Decisive even under pressure, assertive and tough-minded in arguing case, self-confident, shrugs off setbacks.

2. May reserve judgement where uncertain, but stands firm on important points, aims for compromise, fairly resilient.

3. Avoids making rapid decisions, takes an impartial coordinator role rather than pushing own ideas.

4. Doesn't pursue own ideas, goes along with the group, deterred by criticisms and setbacks.

Criteria for performance measures

Performance measures should:

▌ be related to the strategic goals and measures that are organizationally significant and drive business performance;

▌ be relevant to and derived from the roles and objectives of the individuals concerned;

▌ focus on outputs, outcomes, inputs and behaviours that can be clearly defined and for which evidence can be made available;

▌ indicate the data or evidence that will be available as the basis for measurement;

▌ be verifiable – provide information that will confirm the extent to which expectations have been met;

▌ be as precise as possible in accordance with the purpose of the measurement and the availability of data;

▌ provide a sound basis for feedback and action;

▌ be comprehensive, covering all the key aspects of performance so that a family of measures is available, bearing in mind that effective performance is measured not merely by the delivery of results (however outstanding) in one area, but by delivering satisfactory performance across all the measures.

Use of performance measures

The CIPD survey of performance management in 2004 (3) revealed that, in order of importance, the following performance measures were used by the respondents:

1. achievement of objectives;

2. competence;

3. quality;

4. contribution to team;

5. customer care;

6. working relationships;

7. productivity;

8. flexibility;

9. skills/learning targets;

10. aligning personal objectives with organizational goals;

11. business awareness;

12. financial awareness.

Variations in performance measures

The focus and content of performance agreements and measures will, of course, vary considerably between different occupations and levels of management as shown in Figure 4.4. The focus for senior managers is likely to be based on definitions of key result areas that spell out their personal responsibility for growth, added value and results. The emphasis will largely be on objectives in the form of quantified targets, with less prominence given to competences. Their performance will be measured by *what* they do to get results; how they do it will be less important, as long as they avoid upsetting shareholders, the City or fellow directors too much.

The performance of managers, team leaders and professional staff generally will also be measured by reference to definitions of their key result areas. The achievement of quantitative targets is still important but more emphasis will be placed on competence requirements. In some jobs continuing performance standards for certain aspects of the work, which may not be quantified, will be used.

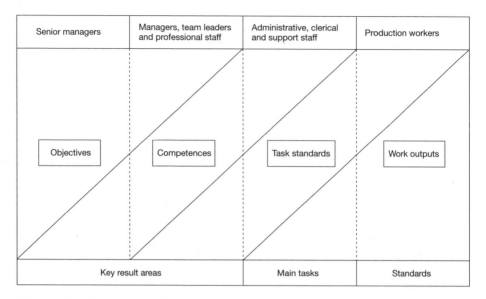

Figure 4.4   Focus for performance measures

In administrative, clerical and support jobs, performance measures will be related to definitions of main tasks or key activities to which continuing standards of performance (role or work objectives) will be attached as the main means of measuring performance. Output targets may, however, be set where they are appropriate, for example number of cases to be dealt with per day. Skill and competence requirements in line with the level of the job will still be important.

The performance of production workers may be measured in relation to work-measured standards for output or time taken with additional reference to competence requirements.

Sales staff are a special case. Their performance is usually measured against sales targets but competences in matters such as relating to customers and providing good service will also be important.

PERFORMANCE PLANNING

The performance planning part of the performance management sequence consists of a joint exploration of what individuals are expected to do and know and how they are expected to behave to meet the requirements of their role and develop their skills and capabilities. The plan also deals with how their managers will provide the support and guidance they need. It is forward looking, although an analysis of performance in the immediate past may provide guidance on areas for improvement or development.

The performance aspect of the plan obtains agreement on what has to be done to achieve objectives, raise standards and improve performance. It also establishes priorities – the key aspects of the job to which attention has to be given. These could be described as work plans, which set out programmes of work for achieving targets, improving performance or completing projects. They also establish priorities – the key aspects of the job to which attention has to be given, or the order of importance of the various projects or programmes of work the individual is expected to undertake. The aim is to ensure that the meaning of the objectives and performance standards as they apply to everyday work is understood. They are the basis for converting aims into action.

Agreement is also reached at this stage on how performance will be measured and the evidence that will be used to establish levels of competence. It is important that these measures and evidence requirements should be identified and fully agreed now because they will be used by individuals as well as managers to monitor and demonstrate achievements.

DEVELOPMENT PLANNING

For individuals, this stage includes the preparation and agreement of a *personal development plan*. This provides a learning action plan for which they are responsible with the support of their managers and the organization. It may include formal training but, more importantly, it will incorporate a wider set of development activities such as self-managed learning, coaching, mentoring, project work, job enlargement and job enrichment. If multi-source assessment (360-degree feedback) is practised in the organization this will be used to discuss development needs. Development programmes associated with performance management are discussed more fully in Chapter 10.

The development plan records the actions agreed to improve performance and to develop knowledge, skills and capabilities. It is likely to focus on development in the current job – to improve the ability to perform it well and also, importantly, to enable individuals to take on wider responsibilities, extending their capacity to undertake a broader role. This plan therefore contributes to the achievement of a policy of continuous development, which is predicated on the belief that everyone is capable of learning more and doing better in their jobs. But the plan will also contribute to enhancing the potential of individuals to carry out higher-level jobs.

THE PERFORMANCE AGREEMENT

Performance agreements define:

▌ *Role requirements* – these are set out in the form of the key result areas of the role: what the role holder is expected to achieve (outputs and outcomes).

▌ *Objectives* in the form of targets and standards of performance.

▌ *Performance measures and indicators* to assess the extent to which objectives and standards of performance have been achieved.

▌ *Knowledge, skill and competence* – definitions of what role holders have to know and be able to do (competences) and of how they are expected to behave in particular aspects of their role (competencies). These definitions may be generic, having been prepared for occupations or job families on an organization- or function-wide basis. Role-specific profiles should, however, be agreed, which express what individual role holders are expected to know and do.

▌ *Corporate core values or requirements* – the performance agreement may also refer to the core values of the organization for quality, customer service, team working, employee development etc, which individuals are expected to uphold in carrying out their work. Certain general operational requirements may also be specified in such areas as health and safety, budgetary control, cost reduction and security.

▌ *A performance plan* – a work plan that specifies what needs to be done to improve performance.

▌ *A personal development plan*, which specifies what individuals need to do with support from their manager to develop their knowledge and skills.

▌ *Process details* – how and when performance will be reviewed and a revised performance agreement concluded.

CHECKLIST – PERFORMANCE AND DEVELOPMENT PLANNING

To what extent have the following requirements been met?

1. Plans are based on an analysis of past performance *and* an assessment of future demands (new skills to be acquired, new tasks for the role holder, changes in the role or scope of the function).

2. Managers encourage individuals to formulate for themselves performance improvement and personal development plans.

3. Plans are finalized and agreed jointly by the manager and the individual.

4. Plans set out clear objectives to be achieved by the individual with whatever support is required from the manager – the plans do not spell out in too much detail how these objectives should be achieved (as much scope as possible is allowed to individuals to manage their own performance and learning).

5. The plans indicate the success criteria – how the individual and the manager will know that the desired results have been achieved.

6. Individuals are empowered to the maximum degree possible to implement the plans.

7. Provision is made for monitoring and reviewing progress without being oppressive.

REFERENCES

1 Levinson, H (1970) Management by whose objectives?, *Harvard Business Review*, July–August, pp 125–34
2 Risher, H (2003) Refocusing performance management for high performance, *Compensation and Benefits Review*, September–October, pp 20–30
3 Armstrong, M and Baron, A (2004) *Managing Performance: Performance management in action*, CIPD, London

5

Managing performance throughout the year

Perhaps one of the most important concepts of performance management is that it is a continuous process that reflects normal good management practices of setting direction, monitoring and measuring performance and taking action accordingly. Performance management should not be imposed on managers as something 'special' they have to do. It should instead be treated as a natural function that all good managers carry out.

To ensure that a performance management culture is built and maintained, performance management has to have the active support and encouragement of top management who must make it clear that it is regarded as a vital means of achieving sustained organizational success. They must emphasize that performance management is what managers are expected to do and that their performance as managers will be measured by reference to the extent to which they do it conscientiously and well. Importantly, the rhetoric supporting performance management must be converted into reality by the deeds as well as the words of the people who have the ultimate responsibility for running the business.

The sequence of performance management activities as described in this book does no more than provide a framework within which managers, individuals and teams work together in whatever ways best suit them to gain better understanding of what is to be done, how it is to be done and what has been achieved. This framework and the philosophy that supports it can form the basis for training newly appointed or would-be managers in this key area of their responsibilities. It can also help in improving the performance of managers who are not up to standard in this respect.

Conventional performance appraisal systems were usually built around an annual event, the formal review, which tended to dwell on the past. This was carried out at the behest of the personnel department, often perfunctorily, and then forgotten. Managers proceeded to manage without any further reference to the outcome of the review and the appraisal form was buried in the personnel record system.

A formal, often annual, review is still an important part of a performance management framework but it is not the most important part. Equal, if not more, prominence is given to the performance agreement and the continuous process of performance management.

THE CONTINUING PROCESS OF PERFORMANCE MANAGEMENT

Performance management should be regarded as an integral part of the continuing process of management. This is based on a philosophy that emphasizes:

▌ the achievement of sustained improvements in performance;

▌ the continuous development of skills and capabilities;

▌ that the organization is a 'learning organization' in the sense that it is constantly developing and applying the learning gained from experience and the analysis of the factors that have produced high levels of performance.

Managers and individuals should therefore be ready, willing and able to define and meet development and improvement needs as they arise. As far as practicable, learning and work should be integrated. This means that encouragement should be given to all managers and members of staff to learn from the successes, challenges and problems inherent in their day-to-day work.

The process of continuing assessment should be carried out by reference to agreed objectives and to work, development and improvement plans. Progress reviews can take place informally or through an existing system of team meetings. But there should be more formal interim reviews at predetermined points in the year, eg quarterly. For some teams or individual jobs these points could be related to 'milestones' contained in project and work plans. Deciding when such meetings should take place would be up to individual managers in consultation with their staff and would not be a laid-down part of a 'system'.

Managers would be encouraged to consider how to accommodate the need for regular dialogue within the established pattern of briefings, team or group meetings or project review meetings.

In addition to the collective meetings, managers may have regular one-to-one meetings with their staff. If performance management is to be effective, there needs to be a continuing agenda through these regular meetings to ensure that good progress is being made towards achieving the objectives agreed for each key result area.

During these interim meetings, progress in achieving agreed operational and personal objectives and associated work, development and improvement plans can be reviewed. As necessary, objectives and plans are revised.

Interim review meetings should be conducted along the lines of the main review meetings as described in Chapter 6. Any specific outcomes of the meeting should be recorded as amendments to the original agreement and objectives and plans.

Two of the main issues that may arise in the course of managing performance throughout the year are updating objectives and continuous learning, as discussed below. The other major issue is dealing with under-performers, and that is dealt with in Chapter 8.

UPDATING OBJECTIVES AND WORK PLANS

Performance agreements and plans are working documents. New demands and new situations arise, and provision therefore needs to be made for updating or amending objectives and work plans. This involves:

▌ discussing what the job holder has done and achieved;

▌ identifying any shortfalls in achieving objectives or meeting standards;

▌ establishing the reasons for any shortfalls, in particular examining changes in the circumstances in which the job is carried out, identifying new demands and pressures and considering aspects of the behaviour of the individual *or* the manager that have contributed to the problem;

- agreeing any changes required to objectives and work plans in response to changed circumstances;

- agreeing any actions required by the individual or the manager to improve performance.

MANAGING CONTINUOUS LEARNING

Performance management aims to enhance learning from experience – learning by doing. This means learning from the problems, challenges and successes inherent in people's day-to-day activities.

The premise is that every task individuals undertake presents them with a learning opportunity, as long as they reflect on what they have done and how they have done it and draw conclusions as to their future behaviour if they have to carry out a similar task. This principle can be extended to any situation when managers give instructions to people or agree with them what needs to be achieved, followed by a review of how well the task was accomplished. Such day-to-day contacts provide training as well as learning opportunities, and performance management emphasizes that these should be deliberate acts. In other words, the requirement is that managers, with their teams and the individual members of their team, should consciously agree on the lessons learnt from experience and how this experience could be put to good use in the future.

For example, a team with the manager as project leader has the task of developing and implementing a new computerized system for responding to customer account queries. The team would start by jointly assessing with their leader their terms of reference, the project schedule, the budget and the results they are expected to deliver. The team would then analyse progress and at periodical 'milestone' meetings would review what has or has not been achieved, agree the lessons learnt and decide on any actions to be taken in the shape of modifications to the way in which they conduct the project for the future. Learning is an implicit part of these reviews because the team will be deciding on any changes it should make to its method of operation – learning can be defined as the modification of behaviour through experience. The team would continue to adapt their behaviour as required and at the end of the project the team members would agree, with their leader, what lessons have been learnt and affirm how they need to behave in the future on the basis of this review.

The same approach would apply to individuals. For example, the regional director of a large charity holds a monthly meeting with each of her field officers. At the meeting, progress is reviewed and problems discussed.

Successes would be analysed to increase the field officer's understanding of what needs to be done to repeat the successful performance in the future. If something has gone wrong the field officer could be asked to assess why that had happened and what needs to be done to avoid a reoccurrence of the problem.

These are examples of project or periodical work reviews. But continuous learning can take place even less formally, as when a team leader in an accounts department instructs an accounts assistant on her role in analysing management information from the final assembly department as part of a newly introduced activity-based costing system. The instructions will cover what has to be done and how, and the team leader will later check that things are going according to plan. This will provide an opportunity for further learning on the part of the accounts assistant, prompted by the team leader, in any aspect of the task where problems have occurred in getting it done properly.

6

Reviewing performance

Although performance management is a continuous process it is still necessary to have a formal review once or twice yearly. This provides a focal point for the consideration of key performance and development issues.

THE PERFORMANCE REVIEW MEETING

The performance review meeting is the means through which the five primary performance management elements of agreement, measurement, feedback, positive reinforcement and dialogue can be put to good use.

The review should be rooted in the reality of the employee's performance. It is concrete, not abstract, and it allows managers and individuals to take a positive look together at how performance can become better in the future and how any problems in meeting performance standards and achieving objectives can be resolved. Individuals should be encouraged to assess their own performance and become active agents for change in improving their results. Managers should be encouraged to adopt their proper enabling role: coaching and providing support and guidance.

There should be no surprises in a formal review if performance issues have been dealt with as they should have been – as they arise during the year. Traditional appraisals are often no more than an analysis of where those involved are now, and where they have come from. This static and historical approach is not what performance management is about. The true role of performance management is to look forward to what needs to be done by people to achieve the purpose of the job, to meet new challenges, to make even better use of their knowledge, skills and abilities, to develop their capabilities by establishing a self-managed learning agenda and to reach agreement on any areas where performance needs to be improved and how that improvement should take place. This process also helps managers to improve their ability to lead, guide and develop the individuals and teams for whom they are responsible.

The most common practice is to have one annual review (65 per cent of respondents to the 2004 CIPD survey). Twice-yearly reviews were held by 27 per cent of the respondents. These reviews lead directly into the conclusion of a performance agreement (at the same meeting or later). It can be argued that formal reviews are unnecessary and that it is better to conduct informal reviews as part of normal good management practice to be carried out as and when required. Such informal reviews are valuable as part of the continuing process of performance management (managing performance throughout the year as discussed in the previous chapter). But there is everything to be said for an annual or half-yearly review that sums up the conclusions reached at earlier reviews and provides a firm foundation for a new performance agreement and a framework for reviewing performance informally whenever appropriate.

PERFORMANCE REVIEW DIFFICULTIES

In traditional merit rating or performance appraisal schemes, the annual appraisal meeting was the key event, in fact in most cases the only event, in the system. Line managers were often highly sceptical about the process, which they felt was imposed on them by the personnel department. A typical reaction was: 'Not another new appraisal scheme! The last three didn't work.' Managers felt that the schemes had nothing to do with their own needs and existed simply to maintain the personnel database. Too often the personnel department contributed to this belief by adopting a 'policing' approach to the system, concerning themselves more with collecting completed forms and checking that each box has been ticked properly than with helping managers to use the process to improve individual and organizational performance.

When Douglas McGregor (1) took an 'uneasy look' at performance appraisal many years ago he commented that managers shied away from it because they did not like sitting in judgement on their subordinates – 'playing at being God'. Norman Maier (2) suggested that for managers to attempt to give negative feedback and help subordinates develop their performance in the same interview led to inconsistent roles.

Michael Beer and Robert Ruh (3) identified three main sources of difficulty in conducting performance reviews:

1. the quality of the relationship between the manager and the individual – unless there is mutual trust and understanding the perception of both parties may be that the performance review is a daunting experience in which hostility and resistance are likely to emerge;

2. the manner and the skill with which the interview is conducted;

3. the review process itself – its purpose, methodology and documentation.

This chapter explores the issues that need to be resolved in handling these difficulties and the approaches that can be used to conduct effective reviews. It ends with a discussion of self-assessment as part of the review process.

PERFORMANCE REVIEW ISSUES

The main issues concerning performance reviews are:

▮ Why have them at all?

▮ If they are necessary, what are the objectives of reviewing performance?

▮ What are the organizational issues?

▮ On *whom* should performance reviews focus?

▮ On *what* should they focus?

▮ What criteria should be used to review performance?

▮ What impact does management style make on performance reviews?

▮ What skills are required to conduct reviews and how can they be developed?

▮ How can both negative and positive elements be handled?

▮ How can reviews be used to promote good communications?

▮ How should the outputs of review meetings be handled?

- ▊ To what extent is past performance a guide to future potential?
- ▊ When should reviews take place?
- ▊ What are the main problems in conducting reviews and how can they be overcome?
- ▊ How can their effectiveness be evaluated?

Why have performance reviews?

The answer to this question is, of course, that managers have no choice. Reviewing performance is an inherent part of their role. The question should be rephrased as: 'Are formal reviews necessary as a performance management activity to supplement the continuous informal process of monitoring performance?'

The argument for a formal review is that it provides a focal point for the consideration of key performance, motivational and development issues. It is a means for considering the future in the light of an understanding of the past. It answers the two fundamental questions of 'Where have we got to?' and 'Where are we going?' It gives managers with their teams and the individual members of their staff the opportunity to pause after the hurly-burly of everyday life and reflect on the key issues of personal development and performance improvement. It is a means of ensuring that two-way communication on issues concerning work can take place, and it provides the basis for future work and development plans. Formal reviews do not supplement informal or interim progress reviews but they can complement and enhance them and therefore have an important part to play in performance management. In a sense, they are stock-taking exercises that take note of what has been happening in order to plan what is going to happen. A formal review is also necessary if performance has to be rated for performance-related pay purposes.

Objectives of performance reviews

The objectives of reviewing performance are as follows:

- ▊ *Planning* – to provide the basis for reformulating the performance agreement and the performance and development plans incorporated in it.
- ▊ *Motivation* – to provide positive feedback, recognition, praise and opportunities for growth; to clarify expectations; to empower people by

encouraging them to take control over their own performance, learning and development.

▌ *Learning and development* – to provide a basis for self-managed learning and the development through coaching and other learning activities of the abilities relevant to both the current role and any future role the employee may have the potential to carry out. Note that learning and development includes focusing on the current role, enabling people to enlarge and enrich the range of their responsibilities and the skills they require and be rewarded accordingly. This aspect of role development is even more important in flatter organizations where career ladders have shortened and where lateral progression is likely to be the best route forward.

▌ *Communication* – to serve as a two-way channel for communication about roles, expectations (objectives and competence requirements), relationships, work problems and aspirations.

Reviews can also provide the basis for assessing performance especially if ratings are required for performance- or contribution-related pay although there are arguments against over-mechanistic rating procedures (assessment and rating are discussed in Chapter 7).

ORGANIZATIONAL ISSUES

To have any chance of success the objectives and methodology of performance reviews should either be in harmony with the organization's culture or be introduced deliberately as a lever for change, moving from a culture of management by command to one of management by consent. Performance management and review processes can help to achieve cultural change but only if the change is managed vigorously from the top and every effort is made to bring managers and staff generally on board through involvement in developing the process, through communication and through training.

If, however, an autocratic style of management is practised at the top and pervades the organization, a more circumspect approach might be necessary. Arguments have to be prepared to handle chief executives who say firmly: 'I set the direction; I decide on the corporate objectives; only I am accountable for results to the shareholders. My word therefore goes. I am not in the business of managing by consent.' Remarks along these lines are not untypical, especially when the finance institutions are demanding a significant increase in the price/earnings ratio or a hostile takeover bid is imminent. The best thing you can do is to argue as persuasively as possible that the achievement of corporate objectives is far more likely if people are fully committed to them, and that such commitment is more probable if people are given the opportunity of participating in setting their own objectives, and even of influencing higher-level objectives if they can contribute to their formulation.

But if this argument fails you may have to accept that objectives will be cascaded down the organization. Even so, performance management can still operate effectively at the level of defining individual objectives and competence levels and reviewing performance in relation to them, and at least it should give individuals some scope to comment on the objectives that have cascaded down as they apply to them. Some managers may continue to take an autocratic line, but others may accept the benefits of the joint approach that is fundamental to the philosophy of a complete process of performance management. This is where the HR function can foster cultural change by encouraging those who are moving in the right direction, pointing out the benefits to the laggards by reference to successful experiences elsewhere in the organization and, finally and importantly, convincing the head of the organization, if she or he needs to be convinced, that the whole process will add value and contribute significantly to bottom-line organizational performance.

In short, when introducing performance management you cannot work against the culture of the organization. You have to work within it, but you can still aspire to develop a performance culture, and performance management provides you with a means of doing so.

ON WHOM SHOULD PERFORMANCE REVIEWS FOCUS?

Many performance management and review 'systems' seem to focus almost exclusively on the upper and lower extremes of the performance distribution, neglecting the core of middle-of-the-road performers on whom the organization relies to function effectively in its day-to-day operations and to sustain itself in the future.

This is illogical because exceptional performance is unlikely to go unrecognized and very poor performance should be equally obvious. From the point of view of both motivation and retention, the majority of employees who are in the middle of the performance distribution should be given equal if not more attention.

ON WHAT SHOULD THE PERFORMANCE REVIEW MEETING FOCUS?

There are two focus issues in performance review meetings: first, on the emphasis that should be placed on performance improvement as distinct from broader developmental needs; second, on the degree to which the meeting should be forward rather than backward looking.

A single-minded focus on performance improvement at the expense of broader issues is unlikely to produce much motivation. The focus should also be on the individual's learning and development needs, bearing in mind that no one is simply being prepared for vertical movement up the hierarchy. This means helping people to widen their range of abilities (multiskilling in shop-floor terms) to enable them to meet the demands of future change and the additional activities they may be required to carry out. In this way employability both within and outside the organization can be enhanced. This particularly applies to the core of middle-of-the-road performers.

Performance review meetings that are used or are perceived as being there simply to generate ratings for performance-related pay purposes will almost inevitably fail to achieve what should be regarded as their most important objectives – to motivate and develop people.

The slogan that should be imprinted on the minds of all reviewers is that 'Yesterday is only useful if it teaches us about today and tomorrow.' The analysis of past performance is a necessary precursor to the preparation of performance and development plans for the future. But the tendency to dwell on the past rather than looking to the future must be avoided if the review is going to make any positive motivational impact.

CRITERIA

The criteria for assessing performance should be balanced between:

- achievements in relation to objectives;
- the level of knowledge and skills possessed and applied (competences);
- behaviour in the job as it affects performance (competencies);
- the degree to which behaviour upholds the core values of the organization;
- day-to-day effectiveness.

The criteria should not be limited to a few quantified objectives as has often been the case in traditional appraisal schemes. In many cases the most important consideration will be the jobholders' day-to-day effectiveness in meeting the continuing performance standards associated with their key tasks. It may not be possible to agree meaningful new quantified targets for some jobs every year. Equal attention needs to be given to the behaviour that has produced the results as well as the results themselves.

THE IMPACT OF MANAGEMENT STYLE

Most managers have their own management style and are reasonably well aware of what it is. If it has worked well for them in the past they will not want to change it in a hurry. But how do managers with a highly directive style adjust their behaviour when they are expected to conduct review meetings on a participative, two-way basis? With difficulty, if at all, in some cases. Guidance and coaching will be required if managers are to handle successfully the potential dilemma of inconsistency between their normal behaviour and how they are expected to behave when conducting performance reviews.

PERFORMANCE REVIEW SKILLS

Conducting an effective performance review, especially one in which problems of underperformance have to be discussed, demands considerable skill on the part of the reviewer in such areas as giving feedback, agreeing objectives, assessing performance and development needs, planning for performance improvement and carrying on a dialogue.

One advantage of introducing an element of formality into the review process is that it highlights the skills required to carry out both formal and informal reviews and emphasizes the role of the manager as a coach. These skills come naturally to some managers. Others, probably the majority, will benefit from guidance and coaching in these key aspects of their managerial roles.

OUTCOME ISSUES

If individual employees who have taken part in performance review meetings are to be motivated and retained, the outcomes of the meetings have to be relevant and put into action. All too often, review meetings have been seen to be ends in themselves. It is necessary to be clear about the range of outcomes that are wanted and can be handled. Besides performance improvement plans, these can include personal development plans, lateral job moves, job restructuring and project secondments.

Almost worse than no outcomes is the situation when outcomes are agreed, written up but not followed through. Raising expectations that are not subsequently met is a prescription for demotivation and disenchantment. Reviewers need to be certain that they do not overcommit themselves or the organization. They also need to be sure about their own commitment, as well as that of the individual, to agreed outputs.

Enacting agreed outputs is a powerful demonstration of the organization's commitment to the individual.

DEALING WITH POSITIVE AND NEGATIVE ELEMENTS

This is probably the area of greatest concern to line managers, many of whom do not like handing out criticisms. Performance reviews should not be regarded as an opportunity for attaching blame for things that have gone wrong in the past. If individuals have to be shown that they are accountable for failures to perform to standard or to reach targets, that should have been done at the time when the failure occurred, not saved up for the review meeting.

And the positive elements should not be neglected. Too often they are overlooked or mentioned briefly then put on one side. The following sequence is not untypical:

∎ Objective number one – fantastic.

∎ Objective number two – that was great.

∎ Objective number three – couldn't have been done better.

∎ Now objective number four – this is what we really need to talk about. What went wrong?

If this sort of approach is adopted, the discussion will focus on the failure, the negatives, and the individual will become defensive. This can be destructive and explains why some people feel that the annual review meeting is going to be a 'beat me over the head' session.

To underemphasize the positive aspects reduces the scope for action and motivation. More can be achieved by building on positives than by concentrating on the negatives. People are most receptive to the need for further learning when they are talking about success. Empowering people is a matter of building on success.

But this does not mean that underperformance should go unnoticed. Specific problems may have been dealt with at the time but it may still be necessary to discuss where there has been a pattern of underperformance. The first step, and often the most difficult one, is to get people to agree that there is room for improvement. This will best be achieved if the discussion focuses on factual evidence of performance problems. Some people will never admit to being wrong and in those cases you may have to say in effect that 'Here is the evidence; I have no doubt that this is correct; I am afraid you have to accept from me on the basis of this evidence that your performance in this respect has been unsatisfactory.' If at all possible, the aim is not to blame people but to take a positive view based on obtaining answers to questions such as these:

▌ Why do you think this has been happening?

▌ What do you think you can do about it?

▌ How can I help?

USING REVIEWS AS A COMMUNICATIONS CHANNEL

A well-conducted review meeting provides 'quality time' in which individuals and their managers can discuss matters affecting work and future developments. They also provide an extra channel of communication.

Properly planned review meetings allow much more time and space for productive conversation and communication than is generally available to busy managers – this is perhaps one of their most important purposes.

There should be ample scope for communication about the organization's or department's objectives and how individuals fit into the picture – the contribution they are expected to make. Information can be given on significant events and changes in the organization that will impact on the role of the department and its members.

One of the objections that can be made to this free flow of information is that some of it will be confidential. But the need for confidentiality is often overstated. If the feeling is conveyed to people that they cannot be trusted with confidential information it will not do much for their motivation.

The review meeting often presents a good opportunity for upward communication. This is the time to find out how people feel about their jobs, their aspirations and their relationships with their peers and their managers. The opportunity a review meeting gives to people to stand back from everyday pressures and consider matters that concern them with a sense of perspective is an important benefit.

BALANCING PAST PERFORMANCE AGAINST FUTURE POTENTIAL

Traditionally, line managers have been asked to predict the potential for promotion of their subordinates. But that has put them in a difficult position unless they have a good understanding of the requirements (key dimensions and capabilities) of the roles for which their staff may have potential. This is unlikely in many cases, although the development of 'career maps' setting out the capabilities required in different roles and at different levels can provide invaluable information.

In general terms, past performance is not necessarily a good predictor of potential unless it contains performance related to dimensions that are also present in the anticipated role.

Because of these problems, assessments of potential are now less frequently included as part of the performance review meeting. They are more often carried out as a separate exercise, sometimes by means of assessment centres.

WHEN SHOULD REVIEWS BE HELD?

The usual practice is to have an annual formal review that provides a basis for a new performance agreement and performance rating, if that is required. Some organizations hold all reviews at the same time, especially if they need a performance rating for pay purposes. The timing of the review can be linked to the corporate business or operational planning programme to ensure that teams and individuals can contribute to the formulation of departmental and, ultimately, corporate objectives and to provide for these team/individual objectives to flow from those finally determined at corporate, functional and departmental levels.

There may be some scope allowed for separate business units or functions to align performance reviews to their own business planning cycle or to carry them out at the time most convenient to them. There is much to be said for allowing the maximum degree of flexibility in order to meet the needs of line management rather than to conform to the bureaucratic requirements of the HR department.

Some organizations have required performance reviews to be conducted on the individual's birthday (or thereabouts) or on the anniversary of him or her joining the organization. This spreads the load for managers but it makes it impossible to fit the review into the annual planning cycle, and this is highly desirable if the integration of individual / team objectives and corporate objectives is to be achieved.

If the formal performance review is spread over the year, but the company still conducts pay reviews at the same time annually, a separate assessment for such reviews will have to be carried out.

Corporate guidelines to managers on performance management often suggest that they should hold interim formal progress reviews during the year, say once a quarter or halfway through the review year. Such reviews could be incorporated into the normal work or project review process (eg the supervisory meetings held by social service departments) or they could be held at focal points as decided when preparing the performance plan.

Managers should be allowed to choose their own times for conducting such interim or informal reviews, although the importance of carrying them out and not waiting until the end of the year could be emphasized in guidance notes and training. To underline the voluntary and informal nature of such progress reviews it is best not to ask managers to complete standard review forms. They should be left to document them as they feel fit.

Some organizations require a formal performance review for new starters at the end of, say, six months or a probationary period, if that has been stipulated.

PERFORMANCE REVIEW PROBLEMS

The main problems that arise in conducting performance reviews are:

1. identifying performance measures and criteria for evaluating performance;

2. collecting factual evidence about performance;

3. the existence of bias on the part of managers;

4. resolving conflict between reviewers and the people they review;

5. defensive behaviour exhibited by individuals in response to criticism.

There are no easy answers to these problems, no quick fixes. It is wise never to underestimate how hard it is for even experienced and effective managers to conduct productive performance review meetings. It was the facile assumption that this is a natural and not too difficult process that has bedevilled many performance appraisal schemes over the years. This assumption has certainly resulted in neglecting to provide adequate guidance and training for reviewing managers *and*, importantly, those whom they review.

The approaches described in this chapter for preparing for and conducting performance reviews can alleviate the problems listed above even if they cannot guarantee to eliminate them. In summary, these approaches are to:

1. Ensure that the criteria for evaluating performance cover agreed objectives (quantified wherever possible), competences based upon proper role analysis and measures of day-to-day effectiveness, preferably stated as standards of performance.

2. Monitor performance throughout the year in relation to performance plans and agreed objectives, performance standards and behavioural requirements (competencies). Ensure that there is feedback at the time based upon evidence (techniques of providing feedback are discussed at the end of this chapter) and record any critical incidents as they occur to assist in an overall assessment of performance.

3. Take steps to minimize bias (blue-eyed boy/girl syndrome), although gender, racial or other bias is difficult to eliminate. If the review process does not involve the delivery of judgements in the form of performance ratings, bias may not appear so obviously but it can still exist in subtle ways. Mentors and training can alert individuals to the risk of bias and assessments can be monitored by the manager's manager and HR.

4. Ensure that both managers and their staff understand the positive nature of the process. Train managers in the virtues of building on positives as well as how to make constructive criticisms (not more than two or three at a time) that are based on fact and not opinions about the employee's personality traits.

5. Encourage a positive approach by managers so that, by using constructive criticism rather than attaching blame, they can reduce defensive behaviour. Briefing for all those involved on the benefits of the process to both parties should also help. Getting individuals to assess their own performance (self-assessment, as discussed later in this chapter) is another way of reducing defensive behaviour.

EVALUATING PERFORMANCE REVIEWS

There is no doubt that in spite of careful training and guidance some managers will be better at conducting performance review meetings than others. So how can their performance as performance reviewers be evaluated as a basis for further training or guidance when necessary?

Traditionally, the personnel department had a policing role – checking that performance appraisal forms are completed on time and filled in properly. However, this will convey nothing about the quality of the meeting or the feelings of individuals after it – they may have signed the form to agree with its comments but this does not reveal what they really thought about the process.

Another approach is to get the manager's manager (the so-called 'grandparent') to review the form. This at least provides the individual who has been reported on with the comfort of knowing that a prejudiced report may be rejected or amended by a higher authority. But it still does not solve the problem of a negative or biased review process, which would probably not be conveyed in a written report.

Space on the review form can be given to individuals to comment on the review, but many will feel unwilling to do so. If the interview has been conducted in an intimidating manner, how ready are they likely to be to commit themselves to open criticism?

Another, potentially more productive, approach is to conduct an attitude survey following performance reviews asking individuals *in confidence* to answer questions about their review meeting such as:

▌ How well did your manager conduct your performance review meeting?

▌ Are there any specific aspects of the way in which the review was conducted that could be improved?

▌ How did you feel at the end of it?

▌ How are you feeling at the moment about your job and the challenges ahead of you?

▌ How much help are you getting from your manager in developing your skills and abilities?

The results of such a survey, a form of upward assessment, can be fed back anonymously to individual managers and, possibly, their superiors, and action can be taken to provide further guidance, coaching or formal training. A general analysis of the outcome can be used to identify any common failings, which can be dealt with by more formal training workshops. Evaluation of performance management processes is dealt with more fully in Chapter 16.

ANALYSIS OF THE ISSUES

Effective performance review training and processes are not likely to happen unless the issues referred to above have been thoroughly analysed. This analysis should be used as the basis for designing training programmes (see Chapter 10) and developing guidelines on preparing for and conducting reviews as described below.

PREPARING FOR REVIEW MEETINGS

Review meetings are likely to be much more effective if both parties – the manager and the individual – have prepared for them carefully. The extent to which detailed preparation is needed will vary according to the type of review. More care needs to be taken for a formal annual review, and the approach suggested below is aimed at such occasions. But the same principles apply, albeit less formally, to interim reviews.

Preparation should be concerned with:

▮ the purpose and points to be covered at the meeting;

▮ what evidence on performance the manager should get ready for the meeting;

▮ what the individual should do to be ready to explain any performance strengths or weaknesses.

Purpose and points to be covered

The purpose of a review meeting would be defined as being to:

▮ provide an opportunity for a frank, open but non-threatening discussion about the individual's performance and learning and development needs;

▮ give the individual a chance to discuss her or his aspirations and any work problems;

▌ focus the attention of both the individual and the manager on objectives and plans for the future (ie provide the basis for the next performance agreement or plan).

The things to do at a review meeting (it is probably best not to over-formalize this list by calling it an agenda) are to:

▌ discuss achievements in relation to objectives and performance/development plans;

▌ assess the level of competence achieved against the headings and descriptors in the individual's role definition;

▌ discuss the extent to which the individual's behaviour is in accord with the organization's core values;

▌ identify any problems in achieving agreed objectives or standards of performance;

▌ establish the reasons for such problems, including any factors beyond the individual's control as well as those that can be attributed to the individual's behaviour;

▌ discuss any other problems relating to work and the individual's relationships with his or her manager, colleagues and, if appropriate, subordinates;

▌ agree on any actions required to overcome problems;

▌ agree on any changes to the role profile in terms of key result areas or key tasks and competence requirements that might be required;

▌ review and revise performance measures (standards) as necessary;

▌ draw up a personal development plan that incorporates self-managed learning activities by the individual as well as coaching, mentoring or training provided by the manager or the organization;

▌ agree a performance plan for the next review period (the performance agreement).

Preparation by the manager

The manager should initiate the main formal review meeting by letting the individual know some time in advance (two weeks or so) when it is going to take place. A period of about two uninterrupted hours should be allowed for the meeting.

The manager should discuss with the individual the purpose of the meeting and the points to be covered. The aim should be, as far as possible, to emphasize the positive nature of the process and to dispel any feelings of trepidation on the part of the individual. The manager should also suggest that the individual prepares for the meeting along the lines described below.

The basis for preparation by managers should be the objectives, standards, competence requirements and plans agreed at the last main review as amended during the year. Achievements should be assessed by the application of appropriate performance measures. Any other evidence of good or not-so-good performance should also be assembled. Reference should be made to any notes made during or following interim review meetings about the individual's performance. Changes in the individual's role since the last review should be noted. Consideration should be given to any changes in internal organizational, divisional or departmental circumstances that may have affected the definition and achievement of objectives. External pressure that may have affected performance and outcomes should also be noted.

The manager should then work his or her way through the following checklist of questions:

1. How well do you think the individual has done in achieving his/her objectives during the review period?

2. To what extent have the actions and behaviour of the individual been in line with competence requirements?

3. How well have any improvement, development or training plans as agreed at the last review meeting been put into effect?

4. What objectives relating to the individual's key tasks would you like to agree with him/her for the next review period?

5. Has the individual had any problems in carrying out his/her work? If so, what sort of problems and what can be done about them?

6. Are you satisfied that you have given the individual sufficient guidance or help on what he/she is expected to do? If not, what extra help/guidance could you provide?

7. Is the best use being made of the individual's skills and abilities? If not, what should be done?

8. Is the individual ready to take on additional responsibilities in his/her present job? If so, what?

9. Do you think the individual and the organization would benefit if he/she were provided with further experience in other areas of work?

10. What direction do you think the individual's career could take within the organization?

11. What development or training does the individual need to help in his/her work and/or to further his/her career with the organization?

12. Are there any special projects the individual could take part in that would help with his/her development?

Preparation by the individual

The individual should be asked to work her or his way through the following checklist, which complements the one completed by the manager:

1. How well do you think you have done in achieving your objectives during the review period?

2. How well have any improvement, development or training plans as agreed at your last review meeting been put into effect?

3. What objectives relating to the key tasks in your present job would you like to agree with your manager for the next review period?

4. Have you met any problems in carrying out your work? If so, what sort of problems and what can be done about them?

5. Do you think your manager could provide you with more guidance or help in what he or she expects you to do? If so, what guidance or help do you need?

6. Do you think the best use is being made of your skills and abilities? If not, what needs to be done about it?

7. Do you feel you are ready to take on additional responsibilities in your present job? If so, what would you like to do?

8. Would you like to gain further experience in other related areas of work? If so, what?

9. What direction would you like your future career to take with the organization?

10. What development or training would you like to help you in your job and/or further your career with the organization?

Conducting a performance review meeting

There are 12 golden rules for conducting performance review meetings:

1. *Be prepared.* Managers should prepare by referring to a list of agreed objectives and their notes on performance throughout the year. They should form views about the reasons for success or failure and decide where to give praise, which performance problems should be mentioned and what steps might be undertaken to overcome them. Thought should also be given to any changes that have taken place or are contemplated in the individual's role and to work and personal objectives for the next period. Individuals should also prepare in order to identify achievements and problems, and to be ready to assess their own performance at the meeting. They should also note any points they wish to raise about their work and prospects.

2. *Work to a clear structure.* The meeting should be planned to cover all the points identified during preparation. Sufficient time should be allowed for a full discussion – hurried meetings will be ineffective. An hour or two is usually necessary to get maximum value from the review.

3. *Create the right atmosphere.* A successful meeting depends on creating an informal environment in which a full, frank but friendly exchange of views can take place. It is best to start with a fairly general discussion before getting into any detail.

4. *Provide good feedback.* Individuals need to know how they are getting on. Feedback needs to based on factual evidence *and* careful thought should be given to what is said and how it is said so that it motivates rather than demotivates people. Techniques of giving feedback are described at the end of this chapter.

5. *Use time productively.* The reviewer should test understanding, seek information and seek proposals and support. Time should be allowed for the individual to express his or her views fully and to respond to any comments made by the manager. The meeting should take the form of a dialogue between two interested and involved parties, both of whom are seeking a positive conclusion.

6. *Use praise.* If possible, managers should begin with praise for some specific achievement, but this should be sincere and deserved. Praise helps people to relax – everyone needs encouragement and appreciation.

7. *Let individuals do most of the talking.* This enables them to get things off their chest and helps them to feel that they are getting a fair hearing. Use open-ended questions (ie questions that invite the individual to think about what to reply rather than indicating the expected answer). This is to encourage people to expand.

8. *Invite self-assessment.* This is to see how things look from the individual's point of view and to provide a basis for discussion – many people underestimate themselves. Ask questions such as:
   - How well do you feel you have done?
   - What do you feel are your strengths?
   - What do you like most/least about your job?
   - Why do you think that project went well?
   - Why do you think you didn't meet that target?

9. *Discuss performance, not personality.* Discussions on performance should be based on factual evidence, not opinion. Always refer to actual events or behaviour and to results compared with agreed performance measures. Individuals should be given plenty of scope to explain why something did or did not happen.

10. *Encourage analysis of performance.* Don't just hand out praise or blame. Analyse jointly and objectively why things went well or badly and what can be done to maintain a high standard or to avoid problems in the future.

11. *Don't deliver unexpected criticisms.* There should be no surprises. The discussion should only be concerned with events or behaviours that have been noted at the time they took place. Feedback on performance should be immediate. It should not wait until the end of the year. The purpose of the formal review is to reflect briefly on experiences during the review period and on this basis to look ahead.

12. *Agree measurable objectives and a plan of action.* The aim should be to end the review meeting on a positive note.

These golden rules may sound straightforward and obvious enough but they will only function properly in a culture that supports this type of approach. Hence the importance of getting and keeping top management support and the need to take special care in developing and introducing the system and in training managers *and* their staff.

SELF-ASSESSMENT

Self-assessment is a process in which individuals review their own performance, using a structured approach, as the basis for discussions with their managers in review meetings. On the whole, people are surprisingly realistic in assessing their own performance, as long as their assessment is not going to contribute directly to a performance-related pay decision. In fact, some people underestimate themselves, which makes it even easier for their manager to take a positive approach.

Structure

The structure for self-assessment can be provided by a self-assessment checklist, which is given to individuals before the review meeting. The following are some typical questions they might be asked to consider:

▋ Which aspects of your job have you done well?

▋ What do you think have been your main achievements during the review period?

▋ Have you had any difficulties in achieving your objectives or meeting performance standards?

▋ If so, please describe them and why you think they occurred.

▋ What do you think could be done to avoid these difficulties occurring again in the future?

▋ Are there any aspects of your job in which you think your performance could be improved by you or with the help of your manager?

▋ If so, how could such improvements be achieved?

▋ Do you feel that you need more guidance in what you are expected to do and achieve?

▋ Do you think you would benefit from any further training? If so, please specify the sort of training you would like.

▋ Does the way in which your job is designed (ie the range of activities you are expected to carry out) hinder you in getting your work done? If so, what changes would you like to be made?

▋ Does your job make full use of your experience and abilities? If not, how could better use be made of your skills?

▌ What work and personal development plans would you like to set for yourself for the next review period?

A problem-solving approach

The answers to these checklist questions provide an agenda for the review meeting in which individuals take the lead and managers respond as appropriate. The aim is to adopt a problem-solving approach. The role of managers is to comment on and, sometimes, add to the individuals' self-assessment. They should avoid confrontation, ie total disagreement with the individuals' opinions, and should preferably ask exploratory questions such as:

▌ Why do you feel like that?

▌ Why do you think that happened?

▌ Have you taken into account such and such an event?

▌ The information I have is that you have not consistently achieved the performance standard for this particular task we agreed last year. How did this happen?

▌ Do you think there are any other causes of this problem?

▌ Are you sure that you have not contributed to this problem?

▌ Are there any other issues or problems you have not mentioned?

▌ How are *we* going to make sure that this problem does not occur again in the future?

This approach enables the review to be constructive. It is conducted on a joint problem-solving basis, focusing on the identification and exploration of the key problems facing the employee and encouraging the employee to think through the issues involved. The manager will provide feedback, but this is constructive feedback in that it is aimed at encouraging the employee to work out for him- or herself what needs to be done, with the support or help of the manager.

Advantages of self-assessment

The main advantage of using a self-assessment approach is that it reduces defensiveness by allowing individuals to take the lead in reviewing their own performance rather than having their managers' judgements thrust upon them. It therefore helps to generate a more positive and constructive discussion during the review meeting, which can focus on joint problem-solving rather than attaching blame. In addition, it encourages people to think about their own development needs and how they can improve their own performance and provides for a more balanced assessment because it is based on the views of both the manager and the individual rather than those of the manager alone.

Problems of self-assessment

Self-assessment can allow employees to take the lead but the aim of the review meeting remains that of achieving an agreed joint assessment and a development plan. Managers have therefore to contribute and, as necessary, add to the views expressed by employees. There is still room for confrontation if managers bluntly disagree, and it may require considerable skill on their part to persuade employees to reconsider their self-assessment. This can be achieved by good reviewers, but it means taking care to handle the situation by asking further questions or presenting additional facts rather than simply expressing an adverse opinion that is unsupported by evidence.

As mentioned earlier, many people can be surprisingly realistic in assessing their own performance, but some will overestimate their abilities and they need to be handled carefully.

There is another issue faced by organizations introducing self-assessment. This is whether or not preparation forms should be completed by employees and given to their managers before the review meeting. If they are, the latter will have an indication of what they will be discussing during the meeting and the problems they may have to address. But employees may feel inhibited if they have to expose their views in writing, especially if these can be interpreted as being critical of their manager. It is probably best to leave the decision on whether or not the form should be given to managers in advance to the parties concerned, rather than laying down what should be done as part of the review procedure.

Requirements for success

Incorporating self-assessment as part of a performance management/review process is most likely to be successful when all concerned fully understand the purpose of self-assessment and both managers and employees understand their respective roles in the review meeting and how they should be carried out. Employees need guidance on how to carry out self-assessments and both managers and employees need training in conducting reviews based on self-assessment, especially on joint problem-solving methods.

Self-assessment is directed to the future motivation and development of the employee and should not be used simply as the basis for raking over past problems, although it should be recognized that the analysis of any such problems will provide guidance on the way ahead.

Clearly, self-assessments should not be taken directly into account when making pay, promotion or disciplinary decisions.

GIVING FEEDBACK

In systems engineering, feedback transmits information on performance from one part of a system to an earlier part of the system in order to generate corrective action or to initiate new action. In this respect at least, performance management has some of the characteristics of a system in that it provides for information to be presented (feedback) to people on their performance, which helps them to understand how well they have been doing and how effective their behaviour has been. The aim is for feedback to promote this understanding so that appropriate action can be taken. This can be positive action taken to make the best use of the opportunities the feedback has revealed or corrective action where the feedback has revealed that something has gone wrong.

Systems engineers design self-regulating systems that generate their own feedback and respond to this information of their own volition. The same principle can be applied in performance management – individuals can be encouraged to understand the performance measures that are available for them to use in order to provide their own feedback and to develop their own plans for performance improvement and development.

Such self-generated feedback is a highly desirable feature of a full performance management process but there will always be a need for managers, colleagues and, sometimes, internal or external advisers to provide feedback based on their own observations and understanding.

Feedback in performance management is positive in the sense that its aim is to point the way to further development and improvement, not simply to tell people where they have gone wrong (negative feedback). But feedback must report on failures as well as successes, although failings should not be dwelt on as matters for blame. Instead, they should be treated as opportunities for learning so that they are less likely to be repeated in the future.

Feedback in performance management is always based on evidence. It refers to results, events, critical incidents and significant behaviours that have affected performance in specific ways. The feedback should be based on fact, not opinion, and should be presented in a way that enables individuals to recognize and accept its factual nature. Of course there will often be room for some interpretation of the facts, but such interpretations should start from the actual situation as reported in the feedback, not from the subjective views expressed by the provider of the feedback.

Guidelines on providing feedback

- *Build feedback into the job.* To be effective, feedback should be built into the job or provided within 48 hours of the activity taking place.

- *Provide feedback on actual events.* Feedback should be provided on actual results or observed behaviour. It should be backed up by evidence. It should not be based on supposition about the reason for the behaviour. You should, for example, say: 'We have received a complaint from a customer that you have been rude. Would you like to comment on this?', rather than: 'You tend to be aggressive.'

- *Describe, don't judge.* The feedback should be presented as a description of what has happened. It should not be accompanied by a judgement. If you start by saying: 'I have been informed that you have been rude to one of our customers; we can't tolerate that sort of behaviour', you will instantly create resistance and prejudice an opportunity to encourage improvement.

- *Refer to specific behaviours.* Relate all your feedback to specific items of behaviour. Don't indulge in transmitting general feelings or impressions.

- *Ask questions.* Ask questions rather than make statements – 'Why do you think this happened?' 'On reflection, is there any other way in which you think you could have handled the situation?' 'How do you think you should tackle this sort of situation in the future?'

- *Select key issues.* Select key issues and restrict yourself to them. There is a limit to how much criticism anyone can take. If you overdo it, the shutters will go up and you will get nowhere.

- *Focus.* Focus on aspects of performance the individual can improve. It is a waste of time to concentrate on areas that the individual can do little or nothing about.

- *Provide positive feedback.* Provide feedback on the things that the individual did well in addition to areas for improvement. People are more likely to work positively at improving their performance and developing their skills if they feel empowered by the process.

REFERENCES

1 McGregor, D (1957) An uneasy look at performance appraisal, *Harvard Business Review*, May–June, pp 89–94
2 Maier, N (1958) *The Appraisal Interview*, Wiley, New York
3 Beer, M and Ruh, R A (1976) Employee growth through performance management, *Harvard Business Review*, July–August, pp 59–66

7

Assessing performance

Performance management is forward looking. It focuses on planning for the future rather than dwelling on the past. But it necessarily includes some form of assessment of what has been achieved to provide the basis for performance agreements and development plans, forecasts of potential and career plans. In addition, a performance management process commonly, but not inevitably, incorporates a rating or other means of summing up performance to encapsulate views about the level of performance reached and, if required, inform performance- or contribution-related pay decisions.

APPROACH TO ASSESSMENT

In his seminal article 'An uneasy look at performance appraisal', Douglas McGregor (1) suggested that the emphasis should be shifted from appraisal to analysis. The article was written a long time ago but its message is just as relevant today, and the persistence of the concept of top-down judgemental appraisal in many organizations suggests that there is still much to be learnt from McGregor in this area, as in a lot of others. He wrote that: 'This [the shift to analysis] implies a more positive approach. No longer is the subordinate being examined by the superior so that his [sic] weaknesses may be determined; rather he is examining himself in order to define not only his weaknesses but also his strengths and potentials... He becomes an active agent, not a passive "object".'

McGregor was also the first commentator to emphasize that the focus should be on the future rather than the past in order to establish realistic targets and to seek the most realistic means of reaching them.

FACTORS AFFECTING ASSESSMENTS

Assessments require the ability to judge performance, and good judgement is a matter of using clear standards, considering only relevant evidence, combining probabilities in their correct weight and avoiding projection (ascribing to other people one's own faults).

Most managers think they are good judges of people. One seldom if ever meets anyone who admits to being a poor judge, just as you seldom meet anyone who admits to being a bad driver, although accident rates suggest that bad drivers do exist and mistakes in selection, placement and promotion indicate that some managers are worse than others in judging people. Different managers will assess the same people very differently unless, with difficulty, a successful attempt to moderate their views is made. This is because managers assessing the same people will tend to assess them against different standards. Managers may jump to conclusions or make snap judgements if they are just required to appraise and rate people rather than to conduct a proper analysis of performance. The 'halo' or 'horns' effect can apply when the manager is aware of some prominent or recent example of good or poor performance and assumes from this that all aspects of the individual's performance are good or bad.

Other problems include poor perception (not noticing things or events for what they are), selectivity (relying on partial data and noticing only things one wants to see) and poor interpretation (putting one's own, possibly biased, slant on information). This can lead to what Michael O'Malley (2) refers to as Type I and Type II errors. A Type I error occurs when the conclusion is that there are no differences in employees' performance when there are. Conversely, a Type II error is concluding that there are differences when in fact there are none.

Overriding all these problems is the likelihood that managers and employees are unsure what good or poor performance looks like and cannot recognize either when they meet them. The notion of performance is a vague one. Is it simply *what* people produce – their output? Or is it *how* they produce it – their behaviour? Or is it both? It is, in fact, both, but not everyone recognizes that, and this results in suspect assessments.

To overcome these problems it is necessary to:

█ ensure that the concept of performance and what constitutes good and not-so-good performance is understood by all concerned, managers and employees alike;

█ encourage managers to define and agree standards and measures of effectiveness beforehand with those concerned;

█ encourage and train people to avoid jumping to conclusions too quickly by consciously suspending judgement until all the relevant data available have been examined;

█ provide managers with practice in exercising judgements that enable them to find out for themselves their weaknesses and thus improve their techniques.

METHODS OF ASSESSMENT

There are seven ways of assessing performance:

1. overall analysis of performance;

2. written assessment (narrative) of performance;

3. rating;

4. forced distribution;

5. forced ranking;

6. quota system;

7. visual assessment.

These are discussed in turn in this chapter.

OVERALL ANALYSIS OF PERFORMANCE

It is sometimes assumed that the only way to assess performance is by a rating system. But organizations are increasingly taking a different view. Only 59 per cent of the respondents to the 2004 CIPD survey (3) used overall ratings. This is significantly less than in 1992, when the proportion of organizations with ratings was 78 per cent Those who do not believe in ratings argue that performance management is essentially about analysing rather than assessing performance. The aim is to reach agreement about future action rather than to produce a summarized and potentially superficial judgement. In practice, an overall analysis is a form of assessment, as it will reveal strengths and, possibly, weaknesses, which indicate where development can usefully take place. Some organizations such as BP Amoco expect managers to reach an understanding with their staff as a result of the analysis, which will ensure that the latter will appreciate how well or not so well they are doing.

Businesses with a performance- or contribution-related pay scheme may disagree with this overall approach on the grounds that ratings are necessary to inform pay decisions. The majority (73 per cent) of the respondents to the e-reward 2004 contingent pay survey (4) depended on performance ratings to indicate the size of an increase or whether there was to be an increase at all.

Even those without such pay schemes like to follow the traditional path of summarizing performance by ratings 'for the record' although they are not always clear about what to do with the record.

NARRATIVE ASSESSMENT

A narrative assessment is simply a written summary of views about the level of performance achieved. This at least ensures that managers have to collect their thoughts together and put them down on paper. But different people will consider different aspects of performance and there will be no consistency in the criteria used for assessment.

Traditionally this was a top-down process – managers in effect told their staff what they thought about them or, worse still, recorded their judgements without informing their staff. This autocratic approach may be modified by giving individuals the opportunity to comment on their managers' judgements. Or, better still, the summary could be jointly prepared and agreed.

The danger is that managers will tend to produce bland, generalized and meaningless assessments that provide little or no guidance on any action required. A study by Kay Rowe (5) of six schemes using narrative assessments found that: 'A few suggested careful thought and a conscientious effort to say something meaningful, but the vast majority were remarkable for their neutrality. Glib, generalized, enigmatic statements abounded. Typical of such statements was "a loyal, conscientious and hard-working employee". Such a statement may well have been true but it is not very revealing.'

Two ways have been used to alleviate this problem. The first traditional method was to issue guidelines that set out the points to be covered. These asked managers to comment on a number of defined characteristics, for example industry and application, loyalty and integrity, cooperation, accuracy and reliability, knowledge of work and use of initiative.. When assessing a characteristic such as industry and application, managers might have been asked to: 'Consider the individual's application to work and the enthusiasm with which tasks were undertaken.' In practice, however, guidelines of this type were so vague that comments were uninformative, because in the main they were about generalized characteristics. This approach is now therefore largely discredited although it lingers on in some old-established schemes.

The second method is to ask for comments on the extent to which agreed objectives have been achieved, to which may be added comments on behaviour against competency framework headings. At least this is related to standards against which judgements are made but the efficacy of doing it is questionable. The only reason for including a narrative assessment is to point the way to future action, and this will not be achieved by simply putting a few comments down on paper. It is better to provide for action plans to emerge from the systematic analysis of performance in terms of outcomes and behaviour that should take place during the course of a review meeting.

RATING

As noted earlier, most performance management schemes include some form of rating. This indicates the quality of performance or competence achieved or displayed by an employee by selecting the level on a scale that most closely corresponds with the view of the assessor on how well the individual has been doing. A rating scale is supposed to assist in making judgements and it enables those judgements to be categorized to inform performance or contribution pay decisions or simply to produce an instant summary for the record of how well or not so well someone is doing.

Types of rating scales

Rating scales can be defined alphabetically (a,b,c etc) or numerically (1,2,3 etc). Initials (ex for excellent etc) are sometimes used in an attempt to disguise the hierarchical nature of the scale. The alphabetical or numerical scale points may be described adjectivally, for example a = excellent, b = good, c = satisfactory and d = unsatisfactory.

Alternatively, scale levels may be described verbally as in the following example:

▌ *Exceptional performance*: exceeds expectations and consistently makes an outstanding contribution that significantly extends the impact and influence of the role.

▌ *Well-balanced performance*: meets objectives and requirements of the role; consistently performs in a thoroughly proficient manner.

▌ *Barely effective performance*: does not meet all objectives or role requirements of the role; significant performance improvements are needed.

▌ *Unacceptable performance*: fails to meet most objectives or requirements of the role; shows a lack of commitment to performance improvement, or a lack of ability, which has been discussed prior to the performance review.

Positive–negative definitions

Traditionally, definitions have regressed downwards from a highly positive description, eg 'exceptional', to a negative definition, eg 'unsatisfactory', as in the following typical example:

A   Outstanding performance in all respects.

B   Superior performance, significantly above normal job requirements.

C   Good all-round performance that meets the normal requirements of the job.

D   Performance not fully up to requirements. Clear weaknesses requiring improvement have been identified.

E   Unacceptable; constant guidance is required and performance of many aspects of the job is well below a reasonable standard.

Positive definitions

An alternative and increasingly popular approach is to have a rating scale that provides positive reinforcement or at least emphasizes the need for improvement at lower levels. This is in line with a culture of continuous improvement. The example given below emphasizes the positive and improvable nature of individual performance:

Very effective Meets all the objectives of the job. Exceeds required standards and consistently performs in a thoroughly proficient manner beyond normal expectations.

Effective Achieves required objectives and standards of performance and meets the normal expectations of the role.

Developing A contribution that is stronger in some aspects of the job than others, where most objectives are met but where performance improvements should still take place.

Basic A contribution that indicates that there is considerable room for improvement in several definable areas.

Positive definitions aim to avoid the use of terminology for middle-ranking but entirely acceptable performers such as 'satisfactory' or 'competent' that seem to be damning people with faint praise.

Some organizations use the term 'improvable' for the 'basic' category on this list. Others have included 'learner/achiever' or 'unproven/too soon to tell' categories for new entrants to a grade for whom it is too early to give a realistic assessment.

This scale deliberately avoids including an 'unacceptable' rating or its equivalent on the grounds that if someone's performance is totally unacceptable and unimprovable this should have been identified during the continuous process of performance management and corrective action initiated at the time. This is not an action that can be delayed for several months until the next review when a negative formal rating is given, which may be too demotivating or too late. If action at the time fails to remedy the problem the employee may be dealt with under a capability procedure and the normal performance review suspended unless and until the problem is overcome. However, the capability procedure should still provide for performance reviews to assess the extent to which the requirements set out in the informal or formal warnings have been met. Note also that in order to dispel any unfortunate associations with other systems such as school reports, this 'positive' scale does not include alphabetic or numerical ratings.

Number of rating levels

There is a choice of the number of levels – there can be three, four, five or even six levels as described below.

Three-level scales

Three-level scales may be constructed by reference to such terms as:

▌ *overall achievement* – 'exceptional', 'acceptable', 'not fully acceptable';

▌ *achievement of objectives* – 'exceeds', 'meets', 'fails to meet';

▌ *capability/competence* – 'highly capable/competent', 'fully capable/competent', 'less than fully capable/competent';

▌ *spread of ability* – 'above average', 'average', 'below average' (not a desirable approach because it 'labels' people).

Advocates of three grades contend that people are not capable of making any finer distinctions between performance levels. They know the really good and poor performers when they see them and have no difficulty in placing the majority where they belong, ie in the middle category. The following is an example of a three-category scheme used by a large financial services company in which the definitions of levels are more comprehensive than usual:

Fulfilling expectations

In order to fulfil the expectations agreed for your role, you and your manager will agree at your review how you have:

▌ worked with others and developed yourself;

▌ followed through processes and made improvements;

▌ met the needs of internal/external customers;

▌ achieved key financial and business results.

The expectations are stretching and demanding and if you achieve them you will have done well and made a full and balanced contribution that has delivered the requirements of the business.

The majority of staff achieve what we expect of them and are currently assessed at this level – we expect this to continue in the future.

Exceeding expectations

People who exceed the expectations agreed for their role will be exceptional for two reasons:

▌ expectations of all of us are generally stretching and rise over time, so to have exceeded them denotes an approach that has added value beyond these normal high standards;

▌ performance is assessed not only in the job but also compared to colleagues doing similar jobs, so a clearly differentiated contribution will have been made.

People who exceed expectations can therefore expect higher pay awards and faster salary progression.

Not fulfilling expectations

We hope that there will not be many people who do not fulfil expectations. Such people will be counselled and supported to improve their performance but if, in the end, their contribution has not met the requirements of the business they can expect to receive a smaller pay rise or no pay rise at all.

Those who want more than three grades take the diametrically opposite but probably equally subjective view that raters *do* want to make finer distinctions and feel uncomfortable at dividing people into superior (average or above average) sheep and inferior (below average) goats. They prefer intermediate categories in a five-point scale as described below or a wider range of choice in a four- or six-point scale.

The advocates of a larger number of points on the scale also claim that this assists in making the finer distinctions required in a performance-related pay system. But this argument is only sustainable if it is reasonably certain that managers are capable of making such fine distinctions (and there is no evidence that they can) and, where relevant, that these can be equitably reflected in meaningful pay increase differentials.

A variation of a three-level rating approach is used by AEGON UK where each grade in their pay structure has three zones, which define requirements as follows:

1. *Learning zone* (75–90 per cent of target rate): individuals are still progressing and have yet to demonstrate consistently their use of the full range of behavioural and technical competencies required for the role.

2. *Competent zone* (90–110 per cent of target rate): individuals are consistently demonstrating full use of the behavioural and technical competencies.

3. *Advanced zone* (over 110 per cent of target rate): individuals are consistently delivering a superior performance based upon their use of behavioural competencies and advanced technical knowledge.

Four-level scales

Four-level scales are sometimes used, often with positive definitions as in the example given above. They provide for finer distinctions than a three-level scale while helping to avoid the problem inherent in five-level scales of rating drift (unwillingness to use the middle or lower categories).

Five-level scales

Five-level scales are the most common arrangement. Typically, they provide for two superior performance levels, a fully satisfactory level and two shades of less-than-capable performance. The rationale is that raters prefer this degree of fineness in performance definition and can easily recognize the middle grade and distinguish those who fall into higher or lower categories. It is also in accord with the typical way in which the normal curve of distribution is expressed where the middle category includes 60 per cent of the population, the next higher or lower categories each comprise 15 per cent of the population and the remaining 10 per cent is distributed equally between the highest and lowest category. This normal curve was originally applied to the distribution of intelligence in the form of IQs (intelligence quotients). It was believed that general ability is also distributed in the same pattern. However, this is a highly questionable assumption, which has not been substantiated by research.

When confronted with a five-level scale, raters can be tempted to over-concentrate on the middle rating and avoid discriminating sufficiently between superior and inferior performers. Alternatively, five-level scales can lead to 'rating drift' – a tendency to push ratings into higher categories. This can only be avoided by carefully wording the level descriptions to ensure that the middle category is used appropriately and by training managers in rating methodology.

Six-level scales

Six-level scales are sometimes used, as in the example given below:

XC Exceptional performance: meeting all objectives and requirements and contributing outstanding achievements that significantly extend the impact and influence of the total job.

EX Excellent performance: meeting all objectives and requirements and contributing some notable achievements beyond normal expectations for the job.

W A well-balanced performance: meeting objectives and requirements of the job, consistently performing in a thoroughly proficient manner.

R Reasonable performance: a contribution that is stronger in some aspects of the job than others and where most objectives are met, but with varying degrees of effectiveness.

BE Barely effective performance: meets few objectives or requirements of the job – significant performance improvements are needed.

U Unacceptable performance: fails to meet most objectives or require- ments of the job and demonstrating a lack of commitment to performance improvement, or a lack of ability, which has been discussed prior to the performance review.

The rationale for six levels is that it gives a wider range and, like the four-level scale, eliminates the tendency in five-level scales either to pick mainly the central rating or to give in to the temptation to drift upwards from it. Another perceived benefit of having six levels is that the core of competent performers who are given a third-level rating (W in this example) are aware that there are three levels below them. This is assumed to have a greater motivational value than being placed in the third of five grades with only two lower categories. But this number of levels presumes that managers are capable of consistently making the fine distinctions necessary, and there is no evidence that this is the case.

Conclusions on the number of levels

The format to use is a matter of choice and judgement. The CIPD 2004 survey found that the majority of organizations had five levels. Some organizations are settling for three levels but there is no evidence that any single approach is clearly much superior to another, although the greater the number of levels the more is being asked of managers in the shape of discriminatory judgement. It does, however, seem to be preferable for level definitions to be positive rather than negative and for them to provide as much guidance as possible on the choice of ratings. It is equally important to ensure that level definitions are compatible with the culture of the organization and that close attention is given to ensuring that managers use them as consistently as possible.

The rationale for rating

There are four arguments for rating:

1. It recognizes the fact that we all form an overall view of the performance of the people who work for us and that it makes sense to express that view explicitly against a framework of reference rather than hiding it. Managers can thus be held to account for the ratings they make and required to justify them.

2. It is useful to sum up judgements about people – indicating who are the exceptional performers or underperformers and who are the reliable core performers so that action can be taken (developmental or some form of reward).

3. It is impossible to have performance or contribution pay without ratings – there has to be a method that relates the size of an award to the level of individual achievement. However, this is not actually the case. Many organizations with contribution or performance pay do not include ratings as part of the performance management process – 23 per cent of the respondents to the e-reward 2005 survey (6).

4. It conveys a clear message to people on how they are doing and can motivate them to improve performance if they seek an answer to the question: 'What do I have to do to get a higher rating next time?'

Problems with rating

Ratings are largely subjective and it is difficult to achieve consistency between the ratings given by different managers (ways of achieving consistent judgements are discussed below). Because the notion of 'performance' is often unclear, subjectivity can increase. Even if objectivity is achieved, to sum up the total performance of a person with a single rating is a gross oversimplification of what may be a complex set of factors influencing that performance – to do this after a detailed discussion of strengths and weaknesses suggests that the rating will be a superficial and arbitrary judgement. To label people as 'average' or 'below average', or whatever equivalent terms are used, is both demeaning and demotivating.

The whole performance review meeting may be dominated by the fact that it will end with a rating, thus severely limiting the forward-looking and developmental focus of the meeting, which is all-important This is particularly the case if the rating governs performance or contribution pay increases.

Achieving consistency in ratings

The problem with rating scales is that it is very difficult, if not impossible without very careful management, to ensure that a consistent approach is adopted by managers responsible for rating, and this means that performance or contribution pay decisions will be suspect. It is almost inevitable that some people will be more generous than others, while others will be harder on their staff. Some managers may be inconsistent in the distribution of ratings to their staff because they are indulging in favouritism or prejudice.

Ratings can, of course, be monitored and challenged if their distribution is significantly out of line, and computer-based systems have been introduced for this purpose in some organizations. But many managers want to do the best for their staff, either because they genuinely believe that they are better or because they are trying to curry favour. It can be difficult in these circumstances to challenge them.

The methods available for increasing consistency are described below.

Training

Training can take place in the form of 'consistency' workshops for managers who discuss how ratings can be objectively justified and test rating decisions on simulated performance review data. This can build a level of common understanding about rating levels.

Peer reviews

Groups of managers meet to review the pattern of each other's ratings and challenge unusual decisions or distributions. This process of moderation or calibration is time consuming but is possibly the best way to achieve a reasonable degree of consistency, especially when the group members share some knowledge of the performances of each other's staff as internal customers.

Monitoring

The distribution of ratings is monitored by a central department, usually HR, which challenges any unusual patterns and identifies and questions what appear to be unwarrantable differences between departments' ratings.

Consistency at a price can also be achieved by forced distribution or ranking as described later in this chapter.

Conclusions on ratings

Many organizations retain ratings because they perceive that the advantages outweigh the disadvantages. But those businesses that want to emphasize the developmental aspect of performance management and play down, even eliminate, the performance pay element will be convinced by the objections to rating and will dispense with them altogether, relying instead on overall analysis and assessment.

FORCED DISTRIBUTION

Forced distribution means that managers have to conform to a laid-down distribution of ratings between different levels. The pattern of distribution may correspond to the normal curve of distribution that has been observed to apply to IQ scores, although there is no evidence that performance in an organization is distributed normally – there are so many other factors at work, such as recruitment and development practices. A typical normal distribution of ratings is: A = 5 per cent, B = 15 per cent, C = 60 per cent, D = 15 per cent and E = 5 per cent.

Forced distribution achieves consistency of a sort but managers and staff rightly resent being forced into this sort of straitjacket. Only 8 per cent of the respondents to the CIPD 2004 survey used forced distribution.

FORCED RANKING

Forced ranking is a development of forced distribution. It is more common in the United States than in the UK. Managers are required to place their staff in order from best to worst. Rankings can be generated directly from the assignment of employees to categories (eg A, B and C) or indirectly through the transformation of performance ratings into groups of employees. The problem with forced ranking, as with forced distribution and other overall rating systems, is that the notion of performance is vague. In the case of ranking it is therefore unclear what the resulting order of employees truly represents. If used at all, ranks must be accompanied by meaningful performance data.

In the United States some organizations have gone as far as adopting the draconian practice of terminating annually the employment of 5 per cent to 10 per cent of the consistently lowest performers. It is claimed that this practice 'raises the bar', ie it is said that it improves the overall level of performance in the business. Evidence that this is the case is unavailable. Michael O'Malley (2), in an article on forced ranking, described it as a 'gross method of categorising employees into a few evaluative buckets'.

QUOTA SYSTEMS

Quota systems lay down what the distribution of ratings should be and adjust the ratings of managers after the event to ensure that the quota in each level is met. They are usually applied retrospectively to ensure that, if there is performance-related pay and increases are driven by a rating formula, the cost of increases is within the budget. In effect, this means that the judgements of managers have been overruled, which is unlikely to make them feel happy about the procedure. Staff also know that whatever comes out of the review meeting may be changed more or less arbitrarily by higher authority. This will destroy any confidence they have in performance management or the fairness of performance pay decisions. Quota systems can completely turn off everyone involved except the misguided managements who institute them.

VISUAL METHODS OF ASSESSMENT

An alternative approach to rating is to use a visual method of assessment. This takes the form of an agreement between the manager and the individual on where the latter should be placed on a matrix or grid, as illustrated in Figure 7.1, which was developed by Ann Cummins of Humanus Consultancy for a client in the financial services sector. A 'snapshot' is thus provided of the individual's overall contribution, which is presented

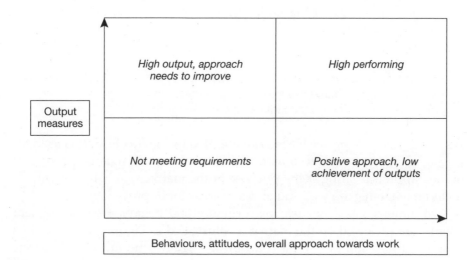

Figure 7.1 Performance matrix

visually and as such provides a better basis for analysis and discussion than a mechanistic rating. The assessment of contribution refers both to outputs, and to behaviours, attitudes and overall approach.

The review guidelines accompanying this matrix are as follows:

You and your manager need to agree an overall assessment. This will be recorded in the summary page at the beginning of the review document. The aim is to get a balanced assessment of your contribution through the year. The assessment will take account of how you have performed against the responsibilities of your role as described in the Role Profile; objectives achieved and competency development over the course of the year. The assessment will become relevant for pay increases in the future.

The grid on the annual performance review summary is meant to provide a visual snapshot of your overall contribution. This replaces a more conventional rating scale approach. It reflects the fact that your contribution is determined not just by results, but also by your overall approach towards your work and how you behave towards colleagues and customers.

The evidence recorded in the performance review will be used to support where your manager places a mark on the grid.

Their assessment against the vertical axis will be based on an assessment of your performance against your objectives, performance standards described in your role profile, and any other work achievements recorded in the review. Together these represent 'outputs'.

The assessment against the horizontal axis will be based on an overall assessment of your performance against the competency level definitions for the role.

Note that someone who is new in the role may be placed in one of the lower quadrants but this should not treated as an indication of development needs and not as a reflection on the individual's performance.

A similar 'matrix' approach has been adopted by Halifax BOS. It is used for management appraisals to illustrate their performance against peers. It is not an 'appraisal rating' – the purpose of the matrix is to help individuals focus on what they do well and also any areas for improvement.

Two dimensions – business performance and behaviour (management style) – are reviewed on the matrix, as illustrated in Figure 7.2, to ensure a rounder discussion of overall contribution against the full role demands rather than a short-term focus on current results.

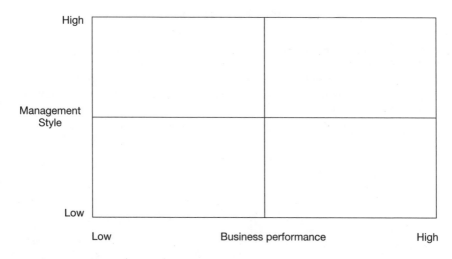

Figure 7.2 Performance matrix, Halifax BOS

This is achieved by visual means – the individual is placed at the relevant position in the matrix by reference to the two dimensions. For example, a strong people manager who is low on the deliverables would be placed somewhere in the top left-hand quadrant but the aim will be movement to a position in the top right-hand quadrant.

CONCLUSION

Assessment is a necessary and inevitable performance management activity but it is one of the most difficult ones to get right. Attempts to use mechanistic methodologies involving ratings or rankings often prove of doubtful value. There is much to be said for the overall analysis approach, possibly supplemented with a visual assessment as described in the last section of this chapter. Approaches to making performance or contribution pay decisions without ratings are described in Chapter 11.

REFERENCES

1 McGregor, D (1957) An uneasy look at performance appraisal, *Harvard Business Review*, May–June, pp 89–94

2 O'Malley, M (2003) Forced ranking, *WorldatWork Journal*, First quarter, pp 31–39

3 Armstrong, M and Baron, A (2004) *Managing Performance: Performance management in action*, CIPD, London

4 e-reward (2004) *Report on Contingent Pay*, e-reward, Stockport

5 Rowe, K H (1964) An appraisal of appraisals, *Journal of Management Studies*, **1** (1), March, pp 1–25

6 e-reward (2005) *Survey of Performance Management Practice*, e-reward, Stockport

8

Improving performance

The improvement of performance is a fundamental part of the continuous process of performance management. The aim should be the positive one of maximizing high performance, although this involves taking steps to deal with underperformance. This chapter deals in turn with improving organizational, team and individual performance.

IMPROVING PERFORMANCE AT THE ORGANIZATIONAL LEVEL

It is tempting for managements to say that poor performance is always someone else's fault, never theirs. But poor performance may be a result of inadequate leadership, bad management or defective systems of work. It is not necessarily the fault of employees. The failure can be at the top of the organization because well-defined and unequivocal expectations for superior performance have not been established and followed through. And effective processes of performance management can provide a valuable means of communicating these expectations.

THE PROBLEMS AT MANAGERIAL LEVEL

Managers, as Schaffer (1) points out, sometimes use a variety of psychological mechanisms as described below for avoiding the unpleasant truth that performance gaps exist.

Evasion through rationalization

Managers may escape having to demand better performance by convincing themselves that they have done all they can to establish expectations. They overlook the possibility of obtaining greater yields from available resources. When they do ask for more they are too ready to believe their staff when they claim that they are already overloaded, and they may weakly take in the extra work themselves. Or they may go to the opposite extreme and threaten workers with arbitrary demands, unaccompanied by specifications of requirements and deadlines for results.

Reliance on procedures

Managers may rely on a variety of procedures, programmes and systems to produce better results. Top managers say, in effect, 'Let there be performance-related pay, or performance management or whatever' and sit back to wait for these panaceas to do the trick – which, of course, they won't unless they are part of a sustained effort led from the top, and are based on a vision of what needs to be done to improve performance.

Attacks that skirt the target

Managers may set tough goals and insist that they are achieved, but still fail to produce a sense of accountability in employees or provide the support required to achieve the goals.

DEALING WITH THE PROBLEM – OVERALL STRATEGY

The following strategy for action was suggested by Schaffer to deal with these problems and get better results:

▌ *Select the goal.* Start with an urgent problem: costs in a department too high; a budget seriously overrun; a quality specification missed; a shortfall in meeting a sales target. Generate a feeling that achievement of the goal is imperative, not merely desirable.

▮ *Specify the minimum expectations of results.* Broad, far-reaching or amorphous goals should be narrowed to one or two specific, measurable ones. Focus energy on one or two sharply defined targets.

▮ *Communicate expectations clearly.* Share with all concerned, both orally and in writing, the nature of the goal, the allocation of responsibility for achieving it, the timetable and the constraints.

▮ *Allocate responsibility.* Allocate responsibility for achieving each goal to one person even though the contribution of that person's team may be essential for success. Ensure that the manager responsible for each goal produces a written work plan for steps to be taken to reach it. The plan should specify how progress will be measured and reported. Then monitor the project.

▮ *Expand and extend the process.* Once success has been achieved on a first set of demands, it should be possible to repeat the process based on new goals or an extension of the first goal.

DEALING WITH THE PROBLEM – HUMAN RESOURCE IMPROVEMENT

Human resource improvement (HRI) is defined by the American Society for Training and Development (Rothwell, 2) as 'the systematic process of articulating organization goals, relating those goals to the performance of people, uncovering the reasons for performance gaps, implementing solutions, managing change and evaluating the direct and indirect results'. HRI is results based, driven by business and performance needs. It works in the following sequence:

▮ Identify an organizational problem.

▮ Articulate a relationship between the problem and human performance.

▮ Determine a quantifiable performance gap between the desired level of performance and the actual level of performance.

▮ Conduct an analysis of the root causes to reveal the reasons for the performance gap.

▮ Implement a series of solutions to address the root causes.

TOP MANAGEMENT LEVERS FOR IMPROVING PERFORMANCE

To improve organizational performance top management needs to focus on developing a high-performance culture. The characteristics of such a culture are:

▐ a clear line of sight exists between the strategic aims of the organization and those of its departments and its staff at all levels;

▐ management defines what it requires in the shape of performance improvements, sets goals for success and monitors performance to ensure that the goals are achieved;

▐ leadership from the top that engenders a shared belief in the importance of continuous improvement;

▐ focus on promoting positive attitudes that result in a committed, motivated and engaged workforce.

The momentum for the creation of a high-performance culture has to be provided by top management They are responsible for developing what John Purcell and his colleagues (3) call 'the big idea'. This is 'a clear sense of mission underpinned by values and a culture expressing what the firm is and its relationship with its customers and employees'.

According to Purcell, strong values provide the basis for both the management of performance and the management of change. These values have to be 'embedded, connected, enduring, collective and measured and managed'. Performance management processes that are aligned to organizational goals and that ensure that people are engaged in achieving agreed objectives and standards of performance and behaviour are an important means of making all this happen.

Top management must therefore articulate and communicate the organization's mission, objectives and core values. They lead by example – living the values themselves as well as ensuring that espoused values become values in use throughout the organization. Top management defines and develops the context for high performance, for example by actively pursuing policies for continuous improvement and by providing the technology, systems and resources needed to meet performance expectations.

In addition, top managers need to provide people with opportunities to learn and to make full use of their skills and abilities. They must communicate to employees regularly to inform them of results, to publicize success stories and to recognize the importance of the contribution made by people at all levels.

The Sears performance model

The means by which a business achieves high performance was modelled by Sears, the US retailing company, as shown in Figure 8.1. This model emphasizes the importance of employee attitude and behaviour in making the firm 'a compelling place to shop' and ultimately 'a compelling place to invest'.

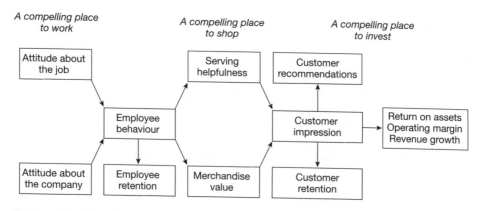

Figure 8.1   The Sears model: employee–customer–profit chain

PERFORMANCE MANAGEMENT AT THE ORGANIZATIONAL LEVEL

The process of performance management at the organizational level is modelled in Figure 8.2.

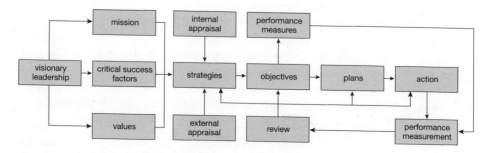

Figure 8.2   Performance management at the organizational level

Mission statements

The start of the performance management process is the formulation of a mission statement. This is a succinct definition of the overall purpose of the organization, setting out clearly what it is there to do and achieve. For example, a software company might describe its mission as follows: 'We are a company dedicated to the development and application of information technology to provide high-value customer solutions that will achieve operational and managerial effectiveness.'

Mission statements:

▌ focus attention on purpose – what the organization exists to do;

▌ convey top management's vision about the organization;

▌ provide a foundation upon which critical success factors can be determined and strategic plans can be built;

▌ lead to the development of explicit statements defining the core values of the organization;

▌ act as levers for change – indicating the starting points for programmes for development, innovation and performance improvement.

It is, however, worth noting that it is more important for an organization to have a sense of mission than a mission statement. It is deeds, not words, that count.

Value statements

The purpose of a value statement is to help develop a value-driven and committed organization that conducts its business successfully by reference to shared beliefs and an understanding of what is best for the enterprise.

Value statements set out how the organization intends to achieve its mission as in the following statement of values for a software company:

How we accomplish our mission is as important as the mission itself. Fundamental to success for the company are these basic values:

▌ *People* Our people are the source of our strength. They provide innovation and intelligence and determine our reputation and vitality. Involvement and teamwork are our core human values.

▌ *Products* Our products are the end result of our efforts and they should be the best in serving our customers. As our products are viewed, so are we viewed.

▌ *Customers* We depend absolutely on our customers. We have to identify their needs and satisfy them.

▌ *Profits* Profits are the ultimate measure of how efficiently we provide customers with high quality products for their needs. Profits are required to survive and grow.

However, value statements are meaningless if management does not practise what it preaches and takes no steps, through the development of supporting policies, to ensure that they are enforced.

It is also necessary to ensure that the values are understood, accepted and followed throughout the organization by defining standards of behaviour and insisting that they are adhered to. Performance management processes at the individual level can make a big contribution to making this happen.

Critical success factors

Critical success factors indicate those areas of corporate performance that are vital to the successful accomplishment of the organization's mission. They describe the key issues to which attention must be given if the organization is to thrive and grow. They could be described as the drivers of organizational performance.

Critical success factors will, of course, vary considerably from organization to organization. The following is an example of the critical success factors drawn up for a small but growing pharmaceutical company:

▌ *product development* – the ability to develop innovative products to meet current or anticipated needs;

▌ *market development* – the capacity to make markets and increase market share;

▌ *process innovation* – the ability to develop new manufacturing processes and systems that will improve productivity and quality and reduce operating costs;

▌ *customer service* – the ability to meet customer needs and to deliver improved standards of customer service;

▌ *human resources* – the ability to obtain and retain high-quality people with distinctive capabilities who will deliver added value;

▌ *asset utilization* – the optimization of working capital, including inventory, and the profitable use of capital assets.

Strategies

Strategies are declarations of intent. They define the direction in which the organization is going in order to achieve its mission. At corporate level they are means of expressing the vision of top management about where they want to be in the longer term and, broadly, how they want to get there. To sum up, strategies are about vision and direction.

Performance management processes are there to support the achievement of the strategies by ensuring that realistic but stretching objectives are set and that action plans are prepared that will implement them.

Strategies may be set out under such headings as:

▌ *corporate strategies* for long-term growth, increased profitability, product-market development, diversification, acquisition, investment and disinvestment;

▌ *marketing* – target markets, market positioning and the marketing variables that will produce the right response in the target markets in terms of new products, pricing, promotion and the development of sales and distribution activities;

▌ *operations* – the future operating resources and systems required in the form of new technology and other systems for planning and controlling production or the delivery of services;

▌ *research and development* – the thrust of research and development activities in the light of assessed market needs and opportunities;

▌ *human resources* – the acquisition, motivation and development of the human resources required by the organization and the steps required to create commitment and constructive and cooperative relationships with employees;

▌ *finance* – the acquisition and utilization of the resources required by the company to its best advantage;

▌ *IT* – the information technology requirements of the firm needed to support growth and improve organizational effectiveness.

Objectives

Objectives can be set out under the following headings:

▌ *financial* – targets for profit, added value, sales revenue, overhead rates, return on capital employed, economic value added, earnings per share etc;

- *product/market development* – projects for new or improved products or services or new markets;

- *operational development* – projects for the development of new systems and processes;

- *performance improvement* – targets for productivity, cost reduction, stock turn etc;

- *growth* – acquisitions, mergers, joint ventures etc;

- *people* – strategies for making the organization a compelling place to work.

Organizational performance measures

It is necessary to measure achievements and progress against objectives, and organizations have therefore to decide what measures should be used. A few key measures owned by more than one function are more effective than a multiplicity of measures – this avoids the problem faced by many organizations of 'drowning in data'. Jack Welch, when CEO of the General Electric Company, followed this precept. He used to say that the three most important things you need to measure in a business are customer satisfaction, employee satisfaction and cash flow.

The key measures are likely to include those concerned with:

- *Financial performance* – for example sales, profits, return on capital employed, economic value added, earnings per share, price/earnings ratio.

- *Operational performance* – these measures will be related to the critical success factors. For example, in a retail store these could include level of service to customers and customer satisfaction, stock availability and stock wastage. A manufacturing company might use measures of quality, throughput, inventory control and delivery.

- *People performance* – for example profit, sales or added value per employee, payroll costs as a percentage of sales, output per employee (productivity), retention rates, employee satisfaction.

The balanced scorecard

The balanced scorecard as originally developed by Kaplan and Norton (4) is frequently used as the basis for measurement. They take the view that 'what you measure is what you get', and they emphasize that 'no single measure can provide a clear performance target or focus attention on the critical areas of the business. Managers want a balanced presentation of both financial and operational measures.' Their original concept of the scorecard required managers to answer four basic questions, which means looking at the business from four related perspectives:

1. How do customers see us? (Customer perspective.)

2. What must we excel at? (Internal perspective.)

3. Can we continue to improve and create value? (Innovation and learning perspective.)

4. How do we look at shareholders? (Financial perspective.)

Kaplan and Norton emphasize that the balanced scorecard approach 'puts strategy and vision, not control at the centre'. They suggest that, while it defines goals, it assumes that people will adopt whatever behaviours and take whatever actions are required to achieve those goals: 'Senior managers may know what the end result should be, but they cannot tell employees exactly how to achieve that result, if only because the conditions in which employees operate are constantly changing.'

Kaplan and Norton suggest that building a scorecard enables a company to link its financial budgets with its strategic goals. They emphasize that the balanced scorecard can help to align employees' individual performance with the overall strategy: 'Scorecard users generally engage in three activities: communicating and educating, setting goals and linking rewards to performance measures.' They comment that:

> Many people think of measurement as a tool to control behaviour and to evaluate past performance. The measures on a Balanced Scorecard, however, should be used as the cornerstone of a management system that communicates strategy, aligns individuals and teams to the strategy, establishes long-term strategic targets, aligns initiatives, allocates long- and short-term resources and, finally, provides feedback and learning about the strategy.

Methods of using the balanced scorecard vary between organizations depending on their needs. At Lloyds TSB, the balanced scorecard blends a mix of financial metrics and non-financial indicators to provide a single integrated measure of performance that focuses on key indicators, from which a true reflection of organization performance can be accomplished. The scorecard thus enables the organization to focus on a small number of critical measures that create value for the organization.

Norwich Union Insurance describes its balanced scorecard as a 'mechanism for implementing our strategy and measuring performance against our objectives and critical success factors to achieve the strategy'. The scorecard is cascaded throughout the organization to measure the operational activities that are contributing to the overall company strategy. The balanced scorecard changes from year to year. Most recently, it set out to achieve three goals: positive benefit, staff impacts, financial performance – in short, service, morale and profits. Previously, the emphasis was predominantly on profit, in order to deliver the promises made to the City and shareholders, but the company feels that more focus is now needed on service and morale.

Plan, action, measurement and review

Performance management is a matter of developing plans to achieve objectives, putting them into action, measuring and obtaining feedback on results and reviewing achievements in order to modify plans or take corrective action as necessary.

IMPROVING TEAM PERFORMANCE

A performance management approach to teamwork can be used to improve team performance as described below.

Setting objectives

Team objectives can be concerned either with the achievement of work targets and standards or with the way in which the team operates.

Work objectives

Work objectives for teams are formulated in the same way as individual objectives. They may be related to the mission and overall objectives of the organization and the function, unit or department in which the team operates. Or they may be concerned with a specific project or area of activity that is not catered for separately in the objectives of any one department but will be supporting the attainment of an overarching objective of the organization, the unit or the function.

The team should agree on its overall mission or purpose and then on the specific objectives that will support the accomplishment of that mission.

In some cases team objectives will be completely integrated with organizational or functional/departmental objectives, depending on the nature of the team. In these circumstances the team could make a major contribution to the formulation of overall objectives and would thus play a positive and active part in an upwardly directed objective-setting process.

There is much to be said for a team getting together to discuss and agree its objectives before the objectives of individual team members are agreed. The discussion of team objectives can clarify the contribution that individual team members are expected to make and the agreement of integrated objectives for the latter is facilitated because they will already have participated in team discussions.

Team objectives could be set out as targets or performance standards to attain or projects to be completed by a certain time and to an agreed standard.

Team working objectives

Team working objectives could be agreed on such matters as working together, contribution of team members, decision making and getting into action.

Work plans

It is important for teams to get together to create plans for achieving their agreed objectives. Work plans will specify programmes (staged as necessary), priorities, responsibilities, timetables, budgets and arrangements for monitoring performance, feedback and holding progress meetings. It can also be useful for the team to discuss its critical success factors – what must be done and how it must be done if its mission and objectives are to be attained. Teams that are closely involved in setting objectives, monitor their own performance against those objectives and take action to deal with problems without referring to a higher authority could be regarded as self-managed teams. And it is for this type of team that performance management processes are most appropriate.

Team performance reviews

Team performance review meetings analyse and assess feedback and control information on their joint achievements against objectives and work plans.

The agenda for such a meeting could be as follows:

1. *General review* of the progress of the team as a whole.

2. *Work review* – the results obtained by the team and how well it has worked together.

3. *Group problem-solving* – an analysis of reasons for any major problems and agreement of steps to be taken to solve them or to avoid their reoccurrence in the future.

4. *Updating of objectives and work plans* – review of new requirements, and amendment and updating of objectives and work plans.

IMPROVING INDIVIDUAL PERFORMANCE

The University of Bath People and Performance Model (Purcell and colleagues, 3) states that performance is a function of ability + motivation + opportunity. To improve performance, therefore, attention has to be paid to:

▌ *increasing ability* by recruitment (people will want to join the organization), selection (choosing the right people) and learning and developing (people will want to enhance their knowledge and skills);

▌ *increasing motivation* by the provision of extrinsic and intrinsic rewards;

▌ *increasing opportunity* by providing people with the opportunity to use, practise and develop their skills.

John Purcell and his Bath University colleagues (3) noted that the opportunity to engage in discretionary behaviour is crucial if employees are to perform well. Discretionary behaviour takes place when employees exercise choice on the range of tasks to be done and how they do their work, covering such aspects as effort, speed, care, attention to quality, customer service, innovation and style of job delivery. People exercising discretionary behaviour are more likely to engage in making their job bigger by taking on more responsibility and doing extra things. Employers may define the sort of everyday behaviour they want but have to rely on their employees to deliver. The Bath team pointed out that: 'Managing performance through people means finding ways to induce employees to work better or more effectively by triggering the discretionary behaviour that is required... This happens when people find their jobs satisfying, they feel motivated and they are committed to their employer in the sense of wishing to stay working for the organization in the foreseeable future.'

Much of what needs to be done to improve individual performance happens at the organizational level. It is about developing a performance culture, providing leadership, creating the right working environment and generally adopting 'the big idea' as explained earlier in this chapter. It is necessary to create what Jake Reynolds (5) calls a 'growth medium' by developing organizational practices that raise commitment amongst employees and 'give employees a sense of purpose in the workplace, grant employees opportunities to act upon their commitment, and offer practical support to learning'.

At the individual level, improvement in performance can also be achieved through policies and practices designed to increase learning by coaching, mentoring and self-managed learning. Martyn Sloman (6) believes that the aim should be to increase 'discretionary learning', which happens when individuals actively seek to acquire the knowledge and skills required to achieve the organization's objectives.

Line managers play a pivotal role in this by encouraging discretionary learning and supporting it through coaching and mentoring. Performance management provides a valuable platform for doing this. Essentially, the approach covers seven steps:

1. *Select the goal* – establish priority areas for action.

2. *Define expectations* – targets and standards.

3. *Define performance measures* – the basis upon which progress to achieving the goal can be monitored.

4. *Plan* the improvement programme.

5. *Act* – implement the improvement programme.

6. *Monitor* – review progress and analyse feedback to ensure the target or standard is achieved.

7. *Extend the process* – continue the development programme as required.

MANAGING UNDERPERFORMERS

Everyone's performance is improvable and the steps outlined above apply as much to high performers as to anyone else. But special action may be required to deal with people who do not meet expectations. When managing underperformers, the advice given by Charles Handy (7) that this should be about 'applauding success and forgiving failure' needs to be remembered. He suggests that mistakes should be used as an opportunity for learning – 'something only possible if the mistake is *truly* forgiven because otherwise the lesson is heard as a reprimand and not as an offer of help'.

When dealing with poor performers note should be made of the following comments by Howard Risher (8): 'Poor performance is best seen as a problem in which the employer and management are both accountable. In fact, one can argue that it is unlikely to emerge if people are effectively managed.' This is another way of putting the old army saying: 'There are no bad soldiers, only bad officers.'

Managing underperformers is therefore a positive process, which is based on feedback throughout the year and looks forward to what can be done by individuals to overcome performance problems and, importantly, how managers can provide support and help.

The five basic steps

The five basic steps required to manage underperformers are:

1. *Identify and agree the problem.* Analyse the feedback and, as far as possible, obtain agreement from the individual on what the shortfall has been. Feedback may be provided by managers but it can in a sense be built into the job. This takes place when individuals are aware of their targets and standards, know what performance measures will be used and either receive feedback/control information automatically or have easy access to it. They will then be in a position to measure and assess their own performance and, if they are well motivated and well trained, take their own corrective actions. In other words, a self-regulating feedback mechanism exists. This is a situation that managers should endeavour to create on the grounds that prevention is better than cure.

2. *Establish the reason(s) for the shortfall.* When seeking the reasons for any shortfalls, the manager should not crudely be trying to attach blame. The aim should be for the manager and the individual jointly to identify the facts that have contributed to the problem. It is on the basis of this factual analysis that decisions can be made on what to do about it by the individual, the manager or the two of them working together.

    It is necessary first to identify any causes that are external to the job and outside the control of either the manager or the individual. Any factors that *are* within the control of the individual and/or the manager can then be considered. What needs to be determined is the extent to which the reason for the problem is because the individual:

- did not receive adequate support or guidance from his/her manager;
- did not fully understand what he/she was expected to do;
- could not do it – ability;
- did not know how to do it – skill;
- would not do it – attitude.

3. *Decide and agree on the action required.* Action may be taken by the individual, the manager or both parties. This could include:

   - the individual taking steps to improve skills or change behaviour;
   - the individual changing attitudes – the challenge is that people will not change their attitudes simply because they are told to do so; they can only be helped to understand that certain changes to their behaviour could be beneficial not only to the organization but also to themselves;
   - the manager providing more support or guidance;
   - the manager and the individual working jointly to clarify expectations;
   - the manager and the individual working jointly to develop abilities and skills – this is a partnership in the sense that individuals will be expected to take steps to develop themselves but managers will provide help as required in the form of coaching, training and providing additional experience.

   Whatever action is agreed, both parties must understand how they will know that it has succeeded. Feedback arrangements can be made but individuals should be encouraged to monitor their own performance and take further action as required.

4. *Resource the action.* Provide the coaching, training, guidance, experience or facilities required to enable agreed actions to happen.

5. *Monitor and provide feedback.* Both managers and individuals monitor performance, ensure that feedback is provided or obtained and analysed, and agree on any further actions that may be necessary.

REFERENCES

1 Schaffer, R H (1991) Demand better results and get them, *Harvard Business Review*, March–April, pp 142–49
2 Rothwell, W (2002) *Models for Human Resource Improvement*, 2nd edn, American Society for Training and Development, Alexandria, VA
3 Purcell, J *et al* (2003) *Understanding the People and Performance Link: Unlocking the black box*, CIPD, London
4 Kaplan, R S and Norton, D P (1992) The balanced scorecard – measures that drive performance, *Harvard Business Review*, January–February, pp 71–79
5 Reynolds, J (2004) *Helping People Learn*, CIPD, London
6 Sloman, M (2003) *Training in the Age of the Learner*, CIPD, London
7 Handy, C (1989) *The Age of Unreason*, Business Books, London
8 Risher, H (2003) Refocusing performance management for high performance, *Compensation and Benefits Review*, October, pp 20–30

9

Performance management administration

It has often been said in this book – but it bears repetition – that it is the processes of performance management as practised by line managers that are important, not the content of the system and how it is administered – and the content often consists largely of forms. The elegance with which forms are completed is not important. Their purpose is no more than that of recording views and decisions; they are not ends in themselves.

Similarly, administrative procedures should not weigh down performance management. It is important to establish the principles of performance management and get everyone to buy into them, but administration and control procedures should be carried out with a light touch. There should be scope for managers to decide on their own detailed approaches in conjunction with their staff as long as they abide by the guiding principles. Performance management practice should indeed be monitored through the evaluation approaches described in Chapter 16. This may reveal the need for individual managers to receive more guidance or training. But oppressive control will only prejudice managers against the process that they will think has been imposed upon them. This is contra to the whole thrust of performance management, which is to get managers and their staff to recognize that this is an effective process of management from which all can benefit.

Performance management is not a form-filling exercise, as many traditional merit rating or performance appraisal schemes appeared to be. HR managers who spent their time chasing up reluctant line managers to complete their appraisal forms and return them to the personnel department often unwittingly defeated the whole purpose of the exercise. Managers tended to be cynical about their rating and box-ticking activities and often produced bland and unrevealing reports that could be prepared without too much effort. They became even more cynical if they had any reason to believe that the completed forms were gathering dust in personal dossiers, unused and unheeded. And, sadly, this was often what happened.

A case could be made for having no forms at all for managers to complete. They could be encouraged to record their agreement and the conclusions of their reviews on blank sheets of paper to be used as working documents during the continuing process of managing performance throughout the year.

But there is much to be said for having a format that can help in the ordering and presentation of plans and comments and act as an aide-memoire for reference during the year. And the mere existence of a form or a set of forms does demonstrate that this is a process that managers and their staff are expected to take seriously. This chapter considers traditional methods of documentation and at the end refers also to web-enabled performance management.

PURPOSE

Before designing performance management forms it is necessary to be quite clear about their purpose. The following questions need to be answered:

1. To what extent are these working documents for use by managers and their staff?

2. What information does the HR department need about the outcome of performance reviews?

3. How is the quality of performance reviews to be assured?

4. How can employees be reassured that they will not become the victims of prejudiced or biased reports?

PERFORMANCE MANAGEMENT FORMS AS WORKING DOCUMENTS

There is no doubt that the main purpose of any performance management forms is to serve as working documents. They should be in continual use by managers and individuals as reference documents on objectives and plans when reviewing progress. They record agreements on performance achievements and actions to be taken to improve performance or develop competence and skills. They should be dog-eared from much use – they should not be condemned to moulder away in a file.

For this reason the forms should be owned by the manager and the individual (both parties should have a copy). Any information the HR department needs in ratings (for performance-related pay or career planning purposes) or requests for training should be incorporated in a separate form for their use.

The employee can still be protected against unfair assessments and ratings by providing for the manager's manager (the 'grandparent') to see and comment on the completed report. These comments could be shown to the individual who should have the right to appeal through a grievance procedure if he or she is still unhappy about the report.

There is, however, a good case for the HR department having sight of completed review forms for quality assurance purposes, especially in the earlier days of operating performance management.

INFORMATION FOR THE HR DEPARTMENT

The HR department may need to know:

▌ who the high-flyers are – for development and career planning;

▌ who are the people who are performing badly – to consider with the line manager what action needs to be taken;

▌ performance ratings for performance-related pay decisions;

▌ recommendations on training to assess any common training needs and to initiate training action;

▌ about the performance of any individual who might be considered for promotion, transfer or disciplinary action.

Another factor that helps to persuade many organizations to hold copies of the review forms centrally is that a decision in an unfair dismissal case may depend on the quality of record keeping as well as the honesty of the performance review process – performance review forms may be required for evidence. This can create a problem if a manager who has produced bland, superficial but generally favourable reports on an employee is later allowed to take disciplinary action for incapability. Employment tribunals do not look with favour on this type of inconsistency. It is always necessary for the HR department to compare review reports with the picture painted by managers when the latter request disciplinary action and to question any inconsistencies.

The approach adopted by most organizations is to require at least a copy of the review form to be held centrally together with a copy of the performance agreement if this contains training and development recommendations. Managers and individuals would, however, be encouraged to retain their own copies as working documents.

It is necessary to remember the provisions of the Data Protection Act, which give employees the right to inspect any documents or records that contain personal data.

FORM DESIGN

When designing performance management forms the aim should be to keep them as simple and brief as possible while allowing ample 'white space' for comments. Like all good forms, they should be self-explanatory, but they may be supplemented by notes for guidance.

Although documentation should be kept to a minimum, such documents as are used should be well designed and presented. A typical form is illustrated in Figure 9.1.

There are many varieties of performance management forms used by different organizations – some more elaborate with, for example, a special 'performance planner' form, and some simpler ones.

They do, however, all have the same basic themes and in some way include spaces for:

- agreed objectives;
- agreed performance and personal development plans;
- review of performance against objectives;
- review of achievements against development plan.

PERFORMANCE AND DEVELOPMENT: AGREEMENT AND REVIEW SUMMARY			
Name:		Forename(s):	
Job title:		Department:	
Reviewer's name:		Job title:	
PERFORMANCE AND DEVELOPMENT AGREEMENT			
Objectives		Performance measures	
Competencies		Agreed actions	
PERSONAL DEVELOPMENT PLAN			
Development need	How it is to be met	Action by whom	Target completion date
PERFORMANCE AND DEVELOPMENT REVIEW			
Objectives		Achievements	
Competencies		Actions taken	
Development needs		Actions taken	
Comments by reviewer:			
Signed:		Date:	
Comments by reviewee:			
Signed:		Date:	

Figure 9.1   Performance management form

If a competency framework exists, the form may include a section listing the competencies with space for comments.

Forms in organizations with performance-related pay (PRP) will often have an overall rating section. Those without PRP may still retain ratings as a means of summarizing performance.

WEB-ENABLED PERFORMANCE MANAGEMENT

Web-based software can make it easy for managers and employees to record role profiles and performance agreements including performance improvement and personal development plans and objectives, monitor progress against the plans, access online performance documents, and gather multi-source (360-degree appraisal) comments. All these data can be used to assist in performance reviews and record further agreements emerging from the reviews. The aim is to reduce paperwork and simplify the process.

The Raytheon web-enabled system is used as the basis for their performance development scheme described in Chapter 2. It incorporates a 'performance screen' and a 'performance and development summary' as well as 360-degree assessment tools and details of how the Raytheon compensation system works. It enables goals to be cascaded down through the organization, although employees can initiate the goal-setting process using the performance screen as a tool. Employees can then document their accomplishments against their goals on their performance screen.

10

Performance management and learning

Throughout this book it has been emphasized that the primary purpose of performance management is to improve performance by developing the capacity to work effectively. This is the all-important learning and developmental aspect of performance management. It takes place at every point in the cycle: planning, managing performance throughout the year and monitoring and reviewing outcomes. It could therefore be regarded as a natural process but the likelihood of its happening is increased if there is a framework for personal development, which is provided by personal development plans as part of the overall planning and implementation activities. This chapter starts with a discussion of how people learn through performance management and this leads to an analysis of the learning opportunities. It concludes with a description of two key learning activities: personal development planning and coaching.

HELPING PEOPLE TO LEARN THROUGH PERFORMANCE MANAGEMENT

Jake Reynolds (1) makes the important point that: 'Improvement and learning are causally related; obtain the will to improve and the process of learning will follow.' He also believes that 'The experience of work always will provide the richest learning laboratory.' This is where performance management has a key role to play: first by specifically helping people to appreciate the need for improvement and where and how it should take place, and second by ensuring that they learn from experience. Performance management can also help to identify specific training needs that can be satisfied by formal courses on- or off-the-job. But the most important contribution of performance management is the help it provides to the development of a climate for learning (Reynolds's 'growth culture'). This offers scope for guiding people through their work challenges, ensuring that they have the time and resources required to learn and, crucially, giving them the feedback and support they need to learn.

LEARNING OPPORTUNITIES

Performance management provides learning opportunities during its three main stages: performance agreement and planning, managing performance throughout the year and performance review.

The performance agreement as a framework for learning

The learning opportunities offered by performance management are based on the initial activities in the performance agreement and planning part of the cycle. This includes a joint analysis of the individual's role so that a new or updated role profile can be produced, which sets out what results are to be achieved and what competences are needed to deliver those results. Discussions take place on ways in which the individual's role could be developed so that it becomes more challenging from the viewpoint not only of new tasks to be accomplished but also the need to acquire or extend knowledge and skills in order to carry out those tasks. The aim is to provide what Reynolds calls 'supported autonomy': freedom for employees to manage their work within certain boundaries (policies and expected behaviours) but with support available as required. Career opportunities and the learning required to realize them are also discussed. Areas where performance needs to be improved are identified and the learning required to achieve these improvements is agreed. The outcome is a personal development plan as described later in this chapter.

Learning throughout the year

Learning is inseparable from activity, and like performance management it is a continuous process. Every task carried out by someone presents a learning opportunity and it is the duty of managers to help people become aware of this and to support the day-to-day learning that takes place. They should enable people to understand how they should tackle a new task and what additional knowledge or skills they will need. Guidance can be provided by asking questions on what individuals need to know and be able to do to undertake a task, leaving them as far as possible to think for themselves but helping them when necessary.

Feedback throughout the year rather than during an annual performance review is also an important means of helping people to learn. They can be asked to analyse their performance and, where it can be improved, come up with ideas about any additional coaching, training or experience they need.

Performance reviews as learning events

Performance reviews, whether conducted formally or informally, can be regarded as learning events. Learning opportunities are provided before, during and after formal meetings. Prior to a review individuals can be encouraged to think about what they feel they want to learn, new skills they would like to acquire and the direction in which they want to develop. During the review individuals can present to the reviewer their views about what they have learnt and what they need to learn. A dialogue can take place in which learning needs can be analysed and a diagnosis agreed on priority areas. Individuals should be encouraged to take responsibility for their own learning and for implementing the outcomes of the learning process. The outcome of the review could be a personal development plan as described below. Following the review, learners and their managers can monitor progress against agreed targets.

PERSONAL DEVELOPMENT PLANNING

Defined

Personal development planning aims to promote learning and to provide people with the knowledge and portfolio of transferable skills that will help to progress their careers. A personal development plan sets out what people need to learn to develop their capabilities, improve their performance and further their career. It provides a self-organized learning framework, indicating the actions required by individuals, their managers and the organization. It serves as a point of reference for monitoring and reviewing the implementation of the plan. Personal development planning is carried out by individuals with guidance, encouragement and help from their managers as necessary. Individuals take responsibility for formulating and implementing the plan but they receive support as required from the organization and their managers in doing so.

The planning process

Personal development plans are based on an understanding of what people do, what they have achieved, what knowledge and skills they have and what knowledge and skills they need. The aims of the planning process are to be specific about what is to be achieved and how it is to be achieved, to ensure that the learning needs and actions are relevant, to indicate the timescale, to identify responsibility and, within reason, to ensure that the learning activities will stretch those concerned.

Plans are always related to work and the capacity to carry it out effectively. They are *not* just about identifying training needs and suitable courses to satisfy them. Training courses may form part of the development plan, but a minor part; other learning activities such as those listed below are more important:

▐ coaching;

▐ adopting a role model (mentor);

▐ observing and analysing what others do (good practice);

▐ extending the role (job enrichment);

▐ project work – special assignments;

▐ involvement in other work areas;

▌ involvement in communities of practice (learning from others carrying out similar work);

▌ action learning;

▌ e-learning;

▌ guided reading.

Action planning

The action plan sets out what needs to be done and how it will be done under headings such as:

▌ learning needs;

▌ outcomes expected (learning objectives);

▌ learning activities to meet the needs;

▌ responsibility for learning – what individuals will do and what support they will require from their manager, the HR department or other people;

▌ timing – when the learning activity is expected to start and be completed.

The plans should be recorded on simple forms with four columns covering: 1) development objectives and outcome expected, 2) action to be taken and when, 3) support required, and 4) evidence required to show that the planned learning activity has been undertaken successfully.

Introducing personal development planning

The introduction of personal development planning should not be undertaken lightly. It is not just a matter of designing a new back page to the performance review form and telling people to fill it up. Neither is it sufficient just to issue guidance notes and expect people to get on with it.

Managers, team leaders and individuals all need to learn about personal development planning. They should be involved in deciding how the planning process will work and what their roles will be. The benefits to them should be understood and accepted. It has to be recognized that everyone will need time and support to adjust to a culture in which they have to take much more responsibility for their own learning. Importantly, all concerned should be given guidance on how to identify learning needs, on the means of satisfying those needs and on how they should make use of the facilities and opportunities that can be made available to them.

COACHING

Coaching is a personal (usually one-to-one) on-the-job approach to helping people develop their skills and levels of competence. The need for coaching may arise from formal or informal performance reviews but opportunities for coaching will emerge during normal day-to-day activities. Every time a manager delegates a new task to someone, a coaching opportunity is created to help the individual learn any new skills or techniques needed to get the job done. Every time a manager provides feedback to an individual after a task has been completed there is an opportunity to help that individual do better next time.

The coaching process

Coaching as part of the normal process of management consists of:

▌ Making people aware of how well they are performing by, for example, asking them questions to establish the extent to which they have thought through what they are doing.

▌ Controlled delegation – ensuring that individuals not only know what is expected of them but also understand what they need to know and be able to do to complete the task satisfactorily. This gives managers an opportunity to provide guidance at the outset – guidance at a later stage may be seen as interference.

▌ Using whatever situations may arise as opportunities to promote learning.

▌ Encouraging people to look at higher-level problems and how they would tackle them.

Coaching skills

Coaching will be most effective when the coach understands that his or her role is to help people to learn and individuals are motivated to learn. They should be aware that their present level of knowledge or skill or their behaviour needs to be improved if they are going to perform their work to their own and to others' satisfaction. Individuals should be given guidance on what they should be learning and feedback on how they are doing and, because learning is an active not a passive process, they should be actively involved with their coach who should be constructive, building on strengths and experience.

Planned coaching

Coaching may be informal but it has to be planned. It is not simply checking from time to time on what people are doing and then advising them on how to do it better. Nor is it occasionally telling people where they have gone wrong and throwing in a lecture for good measure. As far as possible, coaching should take place within the framework of a general plan of the areas and direction in which individuals will benefit from further development. Coaching plans can and should be incorporated into the personal development plans set out in a performance agreement.

The manager as coach

Coaching should provide motivation, structure and effective feedback if managers have the required skills and commitment. As coaches, managers believe that people can succeed, that they can contribute to their success and that they can identify what people need to be able to do to improve their performance. They have to see performance management as an enabling, empowering process, which focuses on learning requirements.

REFERENCE

1   Reynolds, J (2004) *Helping People Learn*, CIPD, London

11

Performance management and reward

Performance management can play an important part in a total reward system in which each reward element is linked together and treated as an integrated and coherent whole. These elements comprise base pay, contingent pay, employee benefits, and non-financial rewards, which include intrinsic rewards from the work itself.

It is sometimes assumed that the main purpose of performance management is to generate ratings to inform contribution- or performance-related pay decisions. Nothing could be further from the truth. Performance management can provide for a whole range of rewards in order to encourage job engagement and promote commitment. These rewards can take the form of recognition through feedback, opportunities to achieve, the scope to develop skills, and guidance on career paths. All these are non-financial rewards, which can make a longer-lasting and more powerful impact than financial rewards.

Performance management is, or should be, about developing people and rewarding them in the broadest sense. Approaches to using performance management to provide non-financial rewards are discussed below. The rest of this chapter deals with performance management and pay.

PERFORMANCE MANAGEMENT AND NON-FINANCIAL REWARDS

Non-financial rewards are provided by performance management through recognition, the provision of opportunities to succeed, skills development and career planning, and enhancing job engagement and commitment.

Performance management and recognition

Performance management involves recognizing people's achievements and strengths. They can be informed through feedback about how well they are performing by reference to achievements and behaviours. They can be thanked, formally and informally, for what they have done. They can be helped to understand how they can do even better by taking action to make the best use of the opportunities the feedback has revealed.

Performance management and the provision of opportunities to achieve

Performance management processes are founded on joint agreements between managers and their people on what the roles of the latter are and how they can be developed (enriched). It is therefore an essential part of job or role design and development activities.

Performance management and skills development

Performance management can provide a basis for motivating people by enabling them to develop their skills. It provides an agreed framework for coaching and support to enhance and focus learning.

Performance management and career planning

Performance management reviews provide opportunities to discuss the direction in which the careers of individuals are going and what they can do – with the help of the organization – to ensure that they follow the best career path for themselves and the organization.

Performance management and job engagement

People are engaged with their jobs when they have an interest in what they do and a sense of excitement in their work. This can be created by performance management when it concentrates on intrinsic motivating factors such as taking responsibility for job outcomes, job satisfaction, achievement and fulfilment of personal goals and objectives.

Performance management and commitment

One of the prime aims of performance management is to promote commitment to the organization and its goals by integrating individual and organizational objectives.

PERFORMANCE MANAGEMENT AND PAY

Performance management is not inevitably associated with pay, although this is often assumed to be the case. Only 42 per cent of respondents to the CIPD 2003/04 survey (1) with performance management had contingent pay.

However, those with contingent pay must have a means of deciding on increases and this has to be based on some form of assessment. The most typical approach is the generation of ratings following performance reviews as described in Chapter 6: 73 per cent of respondents to the 2004 e-reward survey (2) adopted this approach. Ratings can be used to inform contingent pay decisions, often through a formula such as a pay matrix as illustrated in Figure 11.1.

This relates pay increases to a rating and the position of the individual in the pay range. Pay progression is typically planned to decelerate through the range on the grounds that pay increases should be higher during the earlier period in a job when the highest levels of learning take place. A large

Percentage pay increase according to performance rating and position in pay range (compa-ratio)				
	Position in pay range			
Rating	80 – 90%	91 – 100%	101 – 110%	111 – 120%
Excellent	12%	10%	8%	6%
Very effective	10%	8%	6%	4%
Effective	6%	4%	3%	0
Developing	4%	3%	0	0
Ineligible	0	0	0	0

Figure 11.1 A pay matrix

proportion of organizations (40 per cent of respondents to the 2004 e-reward survey) use this somewhat mechanistic approach.

But quite a few organizations do not use ratings at all (27 per cent of the e-reward respondents). Instead they adopt what might be called 'holistic' assessment. This involves assessing the level of contribution and therefore possible awards in the shape of base pay increases or bonuses. Consideration is given both to what individuals have contributed to the success of their team and to the level of competence they have achieved and deployed. Team members who are contributing at the expected level will be paid at or around what is often called 'the reference point' for the grade (a reference point represents the rate of pay appropriate for someone who is fully competent in the role and will be aligned to market rates in accordance with the organization's market pay policies). If, in the judgement of the line manager, individuals are achieving this level of contribution but are paid below their peers at the reference point, the pay of such individuals would be brought up to the level of their peers or towards that level if it is felt that the increase should be phased. Individuals may be paid above the reference point if they are making a particularly strong contribution or if their market worth is higher.

The policy guideline would be that the average pay of those in the grade should broadly be in line with the reference point unless there are special market rate considerations that justify a higher rate. Those at or above the reference point who are contributing well could be eligible for a cash bonus. A 'pay pot' would be made available for distribution with guidelines on how it should be used.

This approach depends largely on the judgement of line managers, although they would be guided and helped in the exercise of that judgement by HR. Its acceptability to staff as a fair process depends on precise communications generally on how it operates and equally precise communications individually on why decisions have been made. The assessment of contribution should be a joint one as part of performance management and the link between that assessment and the pay decision should be clear.

The method used at Halifax BOS was described by Julie Hill, HR Partner, Retail Sales as follows:

We look at a number of things when making a decision on an individual's pay. One will be the size of the role as determined by job evaluation and we also consider market data and location to determine the average salary that you would expect to pay for that role. We then look at how the individual has performed over the last 12 months: Have they contributed what was expected of them? Have they contributed above and beyond their peers? Have they underperformed in respect of what was required of them? These are not ratings; they are just guidelines given to managers as to whether the individual should be given an average, above-average or below-average increase. We have a devolved budget and managers have to make decisions as to what percentage they should give to different people. We suggest that if, for example, a manager has six people carrying out the same roles then, from an equal pay point of view, if they are delivering at the same level and are all competent, they should be getting similar salaries. Individuals paid below the market rate who are performing effectively may get a bigger pay rise to bring them nearer the market rate for the role.

Reconciling performance management and pay

Focusing on performance management as a means of deciding on pay awards may conflict with the developmental purposes of performance management. This is likely to be the case if ratings are used – the performance review meeting will concentrate on the ratings that emerge from it and how much money will be forthcoming. Issues concerning development and the non-financial reward approaches discussed earlier will be subordinated to this preoccupation with pay. Many organizations attempt to get over this problem by holding development and pay review meetings on separate dates, often several months apart (decoupling). Some such as Halifax BOS as described earlier do without formulaic approaches (ratings and pay matrices) altogether, although it is impossible to dissociate contingent pay completely from some form of assessment.

The problem of reconciling the developmental aspects of performance management or appraisal and pay has been with us for decades. Armstrong commented as long ago as 1976 (3) that: 'It is undesirable to have a direct link between the performance review and the reward review. The former must aim primarily at improving performance and, possibly, assessing potential. If this is confused with a salary review, everyone becomes over-concerned about the impact of the assessment on the increment... It is better to separate the two.'

Many people since then have accepted this view in principle but have found it difficult to apply in practice. As Kessler and Purcell (4) argue: 'How distinct these processes (performance review and performance-related pay) can ever be or, in managerial terms, should ever be, is perhaps debatable. It is unrealistic to assume that a manager can separate these two processes easily and it could be argued that the evaluations in a broad sense should be congruent.' And Armstrong and Murlis (5) comment that: 'Some organisations separate entirely performance pay ratings from the performance management review. But there will, of course, inevitably be a read-across from the performance management review to the pay-for-performance review.'

The issue is that if you want to pay for performance or competence you have to measure performance or competence. And if you want, as you should do, the process of measurement to be fair, equitable, consistent and transparent, then you cannot make pay decisions, on whatever evidence, behind closed doors. You must convey to people how the assessment has been made and how it has been converted into a pay increase. This is a matter of procedural justice that demands that, where there is a system for assessing performance and competence, 1) the assessment should be based on 'good information and informed opinion', 2) the person affected should be able to contribute to the process of obtaining evidence to support the assessment, 3) the person should know how and why the assessment has been made, and 4) the person should be able to appeal against the assessment.

REFERENCES

1   Armstrong, M and Baron, A (2004) *Managing Performance: Performance management in action*, CIPD, London
2   e-reward (2004) *Report on Contingent Pay*, e-reward, Stockport
3   Armstrong, M (1976) *A Handbook of Personnel Management Practice*, 1st edn, Kogan Page, London
4   Kessler, I and Purcell, J (1993) *The Templeton Performance-Related Pay Project: Summary of key findings*, Templeton College, Oxford
5   Armstrong, M and Murlis, H (1998) *Reward Management*, 4th edn, Kogan Page, London

12

360-degree feedback

360-degree feedback is a relatively new feature of performance management although interest is growing. The Institute of Personnel and Development 1998 survey (1) found that only 11 per cent of the organizations covered used it, but the e-reward 2005 survey (2) established that 30 per cent did. This chapter starts with a definition of 360-degree feedback and goes on to describe how it is used and operated and to discuss its advantages and disadvantages and methods of introduction.

360-DEGREE FEEDBACK DEFINED

360-degree feedback has been defined by Ward (3) as: 'The systematic collection and feedback of performance data on an individual or group derived from a number of the stakeholders on their performance.'

The data are usually fed back in the form of ratings against various performance dimensions. 360-degree feedback is also referred to as multi-source assessment or multi-rater feedback.

Performance data in a 360-degree feedback process can be generated for individuals (as shown in Figure 12.1) from the person to whom they report, their direct reports, their peers (who could be team members and/or colleagues in other parts of the organization) and their internal customers.

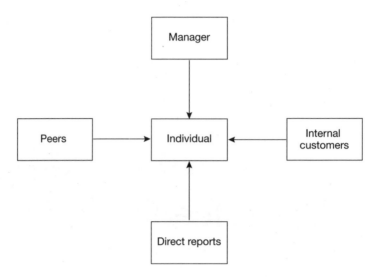

Figure 12.1 360-degree feedback model

The range of feedback could be extended to include other stakeholders – external customers, clients or suppliers (this is sometimes known as 540-degree feedback). A self-assessment process may also be incorporated using for comparison purposes the same criteria as the other generators of feedback.

Feedback can be initiated entirely by peers (in a team setting) or by both peers and the team leaders. It can also take the form of 180-degree or upward feedback where this is given by subordinates to their managers. Feedback may be presented direct to individuals, or to their managers, or both. Expert counselling and coaching for individuals as a result of the feedback may be provided by a member of the HR department or an outside consultant.

USE OF 360-DEGREE FEEDBACK

360-degree feedback is used for a number of purposes. Research conducted by the Ashridge Management Research Group (4) found that, typically, 360-degree feedback forms part of a self-development or management development programme. The 45 users covered by the survey fell into the following groups:

▮ 71 per cent used it solely to support learning and development.

▮ 23 per cent used it to support a number of HR processes such as appraisal, resourcing and succession planning.

▮ 6 per cent used it to support pay decisions.

A 1997 survey of 22 organizations using 360-degree feedback by the Performance Management Group (unpublished) found that:

▮ 77 per cent either disagreed or strongly disagreed with the statement that it is 'a personal' development tool and should not be used for wider HR or organizational purposes.

▮ 81 per cent disagreed or strongly disagreed that 'the natural use of 360-degree feedback is to provide a basis for reward'.

The IPD 1998 survey also found that the 51 organizations covered by the research predominantly used 360-degree feedback to help in assessing development needs and as a basis for performance coaching. Only one-fifth of the respondents used it to determine a performance grade or pay award.

RATIONALE FOR 360-DEGREE FEEDBACK

The main rationale for 360-degree feedback has been expressed by Turnow (5) as follows: '360-degree activities are usually based on two key assumptions: (1) that awareness of any discrepancy between how we see ourselves and how others see us increases self-awareness, and (2) that enhanced self-awareness is a key to maximum performance as a leader, and thus becomes a foundation block for management and leadership development programmes.'

London and Beatty (6) have suggested that the rationale for 360-degree feedback is as follows:

▮ 360-degree feedback can become a powerful organizational intervention to increase awareness of the importance of aligning leader behaviour, work unit results, and customer expectations, as well as increasing employee participation in leadership development and work unit effectiveness.

❚ 360-degree feedback recognizes the complexity of management and the value of input from various sources – it is axiomatic that managers should not be assessing behaviours they cannot observe, and the leadership behaviours of subordinates may not be known to their managers.

❚ 360-degree feedback calls attention to important performance dimensions that may hitherto have been neglected by the organization.

360-DEGREE FEEDBACK – METHODOLOGY

The questionnaire

360-degree feedback processes usually obtain data from questionnaires that measure from different perspectives the behaviours of individuals against a list of competencies. In effect, they ask for an evaluation: 'How well does... do...?' The competency model may be one developed within the organization or the competency headings may be provided by the supplier of a questionnaire.

The dimensions may broadly refer to leadership, management and approaches to work. The headings used in the Performance Management Group's Orbit 360-degree questionnaire are:

❚ leadership;

❚ team player/manage people;

❚ self-management;

❚ communication;

❚ vision;

❚ organizational skills;

❚ decision making;

❚ expertise;

❚ drive;

❚ adaptability.

The leadership heading, for example, is defined as: 'Shares a clear vision and focuses on achieving it. Demonstrates commitment to the organization's mission. Provides a coherent sense of purpose and direction, both internally and externally, harnessing energy and enthusiasm of staff.'

Ratings

Ratings are given by the generators of the feedback on a scale against each heading. This may refer to both importance and performance, as in the PILAT questionnaire, which asks those completing it to rate the importance of each item on a scale of 1 (not important) to 6 (essential), and performance on a scale of 1 (weak in this area) to 6 (outstanding). Ratings may be supplemented by text comments.

Data processing

Questionnaires are normally processed with the help of software developed within the organization or, most commonly, provided by external suppliers. This enables the data collection and analysis to be completed swiftly, with the minimum of effort and in a way that facilitates graphical as well as numerical presentation.

Graphical presentation is preferable as a means of easing the process of assimilating the data. The simplest method is to produce a profile as illustrated in Figure 12.2.

Some of the proprietary software presents feedback data in a much more elaborate form.

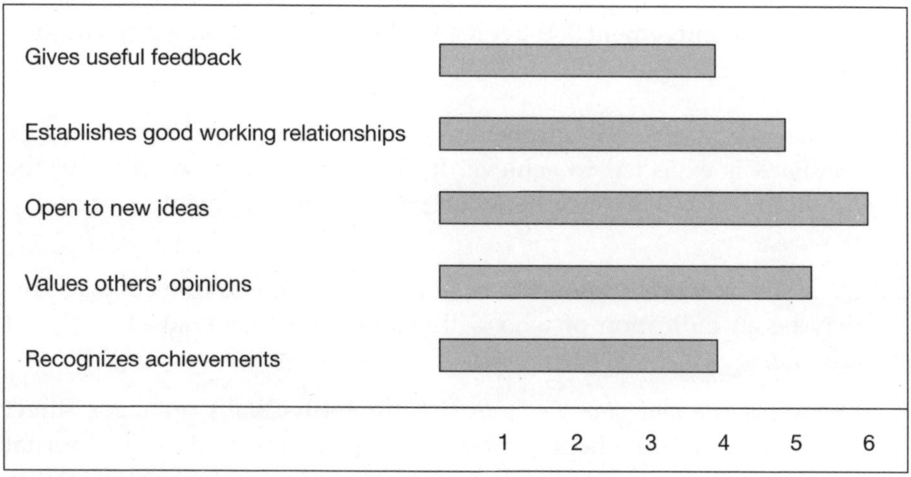

Figure 12.2 360-degree feedback profile

Internet-hosted systems are also available that enable organizations to outsource administration and analysis easily.

Feedback

The feedback is often anonymous and may be presented to the individual (most commonly), to the individual's manager (less commonly) or to both the individual and the manager. Some organizations do not arrange for feedback to be anonymous. Whether or not feedback is anonymous depends on the organization's culture – the more open the culture, the more likely is the source of feedback to be revealed.

Action

The action generated by the feedback will depend on the purposes of the process, ie development, appraisal or pay. If the purpose is primarily developmental, the action may be left to individuals as part of their personal development plans, but the planning process may be shared between individuals and their managers if they both have access to the information. Even if the data go only to the individual, they can be discussed in a performance review meeting so that joint plans can be made, and there is much to be said for adopting this approach.

DEVELOPMENT AND IMPLEMENTATION

To develop and implement 360-degree feedback the following steps need to be taken:

1. *Define objectives* – it is important to define exactly what 360-degree feedback is expected to achieve. It will be necessary to spell out the extent to which it is concerned with personal development, appraisal or pay.

2. *Decide on recipients* – who is to be at the receiving end of feedback. This may be an indication of who will eventually be covered after a pilot scheme.

3. *Decide on who will give the feedback* – the individual's manager, direct reports, team members, other colleagues, internal and external customers. A decision will also have to be made on whether HR staff or

outside consultants should take part in helping managers to make use of the feedback. A further decision will need to be made on whether or not the feedback should be anonymous (it usually is).

4. *Decide on the areas of work and behaviour on which feedback will be given* – this may be in line with an existing competency model or it may take the form of a list of headings for development. Clearly, the model should fit the culture, values and type of work carried out in the organization. But it might be decided that a list of headings or questions in a software package would be acceptable, at least to start with.

5. *Decide on the method of collecting the data* – the questionnaire could be designed in-house, or a consultant's or software provider's question-naire could be adopted, with the possible option of amending it later to produce a better fit.

6. *Decide on data analysis and presentation* – again, the decision is on devel-oping the software in-house or using a package. Most organizations installing 360-degree feedback do, in fact, purchase a package from a consultancy or software house. But the aim should be to keep it as simple as possible.

7. *Plan the initial implementation programme* – it is desirable to pilot the process, preferably at top level or with all the managers in a function or department. The pilot scheme will need to be launched with communi-cations to those involved about the purpose of 360-degree feedback, how it will work and the part they will play. The aim is to spell out the benefits and, as far as possible, allay any fears. Training in giving and receiving feedback will also be necessary.

8. *Analyse the outcome of the pilot scheme* – the reactions of those taking part in a pilot scheme should be analysed and necessary changes made to the process, the communication package and the training.

9. *Plan and implement the full programme* – this should include briefing, communicating, training and support from HR and, possibly, the external consultants.

10. *Monitor and evaluate* – maintain a particularly close watch on the initial implementation of feedback but monitoring should continue. This is a process that can cause anxiety and stress, or produce little practical gain in terms of development and improved performance for a lot of effort.

360-DEGREE FEEDBACK – ADVANTAGES AND DISADVANTAGES

The survey conducted by the Performance Management Group in 1997 (unpublished) revealed that respondents believed the following benefits resulted from using 360-degree feedback:

▮ Individuals get a broader perspective of how they are perceived by others than previously possible.

▮ Increased awareness of and relevance of competencies.

▮ Increased awareness by senior management that they too have development needs.

▮ More reliable feedback to senior managers about their performance.

▮ Gaining acceptance of the principle of multiple stakeholders as a measure of performance.

▮ Encouraging more open feedback – new insights.

▮ Reinforcing the desired competencies of the business.

▮ Provided a clearer picture to senior management of individual's real worth (although there tended to be some 'halo' effect syndromes).

▮ Clarified to employees critical performance aspects.

▮ Opens up feedback and gives people a more rounded view of performance than they had previously.

▮ Identifying key development areas for the individual, a department and the organization as a whole.

▮ Identifying strengths that can be used to the best advantage of the business.

▮ A rounded view of the individual's/team's/organization's performance and what the strengths and weaknesses are.

▮ Raised the self-awareness of people managers of how they personally impact upon others – positively and negatively.

▮ Supporting a climate of continuous improvement.

▮ Starting to improve the climate/morale, as measured through the survey.

- Focused agenda for development. Forced line managers to discuss development issues.

- Perception of feedback as more valid and objective, leading to acceptance of results and actions required.

But there may be problems. These include:

- people not giving frank or honest feedback;

- people being put under stress in receiving or giving feedback;

- lack of action following feedback;

- over-reliance on technology;

- too much bureaucracy.

These can all be minimized if not avoided completely by careful design, communication, training and follow-up.

360-DEGREE FEEDBACK – CRITERIA FOR SUCCESS

360-degree feedback is most likely to be successful when:

- it has the active support of top management who themselves take part in giving and receiving feedback and encourage everyone else to do the same;

- there is commitment everywhere else to the process based on briefing, training and an understanding of the benefits to individuals as well as the organization;

- there is real determination by all concerned to use feedback data as the basis for development;

- questionnaire items fit or reflect typical and significant aspects of behaviour;

- items covered in the questionnaire can be related to actual events experienced by the individual;

- comprehensive and well-delivered communication and training programmes are followed;

▌ no one feels threatened by the process – this is often achieved by making feedback anonymous and/or getting a third-party facilitator to deliver the feedback;

▌ feedback questionnaires are relatively easy to complete (not unduly complex or lengthy, with clear instructions);

▌ bureaucracy is minimized.

REFERENCES

1 Armstrong, M and Baron, A (1998) *Performance Management: The new realities*, Institute of Personnel and Development, London
2 e-reward (2005) *Survey of Performance Management Practice*, e-reward, Stockport
3 Ward, P (1997) *360-Degree Feedback*, Institute of Personnel and Development, London
4 Handy, L, Devine, M and Heath, L (1996) *360-Degree Feedback: Unguided missile or powerful weapon?*, Ashridge Management Group, Berkhamsted
5 Turnow, W W (1993) Introduction to special issues on 360-degree feedback, *Human Resource Management*, Summer/Fall, pp 311–16
6 London, M and Beatty, R W (1993) 360-degree feedback as competitive advantage, *Human Resource Management*, Summer/Fall, pp 353–72

13

Performance management roles

There are four groups of people whose commitment to performance management is crucial to its success: top managers, line managers, employees generally, and HR specialists.

TOP MANAGERS

Top managers take the lead, set the direction, act as role models and define and act upon core values relating to performance. It is their job to convince everyone that they believe performance management plays a key role in ensuring that business goals are achieved. They must demonstrate by their behaviour that performance management is indeed about managing the business. They have to spell out to line managers that their performance will only be acceptable if they take performance management seriously and use its processes to deliver better results.

It is the responsibility of top managers to develop a high-performance culture, which means ensuring that:

▌ they communicate a clear sense of mission underpinned by values, and a culture expressing what the firm is and its relationship with its customers and employees – John Purcell's 'the big idea' (1);

▌ a clear line of sight exists between the strategic aims of the business and those of its departments and its staff at all levels;

▌ expectations are defined and communicated to everyone in the shape of goals for success, performance improvements and core values;

▌ everyone is kept informed of progress towards achieving goals and what needs to be done if performance is not up to expectations;

▌ leadership is provided that engenders a shared belief in the importance of continuing improvement.

LINE MANAGERS

The research conducted by John Purcell and his colleagues (1) led to the conclusion that 'front line management or leadership played a pivotal role in terms of implementing and enacting HR policies and practices since it is the front line managers that "bring policies to life"'. An important consideration in designing and operating performance management is how to achieve this by gaining their commitment and ensuring that they have the skills required. The need is to fill the gap between rhetoric and reality, between what top management and HR want line managers to do and what line managers actually do.

Julie Hill, HR Partner, Retail Sales, Halifax BOS has provided the following illustration of the situation faced by her organization and how it was dealt with:

> Performance management works very well with managers who are competent. Those who are less competent with the behavioural requirements of their role find it difficult, as this approach requires them to make some business judgements and discuss the rationale for them. Previously, they relied on the tick box approach where there was sometimes a perception that they did not need to discuss performance in detail. We have had to do quite a lot of coaching with managers to get them to feel comfortable with the new model as some feel the safety net of the tick box system has been removed. We have introduced role profiles which describe the 'how' and the 'what' and provides something against which managers and colleagues can be measured/assessed.

The problem of appraisals

On the basis of the Bath University research, Sue Hutchinson and John Purcell (2) discuss 'performance appraisal' as an HR activity (they do not refer to performance management as a management activity). They note that: 'Performance appraisal is an area in which front line managers have traditionally had direct involvement with their staff, and provides a good example of the key role these managers have to play in their delivery of HR policies.' They also found that:

> Looking at the sample of employees interviewed over the two years (n=608) we found that performance appraisal was rated as the least effective HR policy (in terms of levels of satisfaction) after pay, and in a fair number of organizations it was the least favourite HR activity. The reasons given were numerous, and included the views that the measurements and targets were felt to be unclear and/or not relevant, and that the system was too complicated and time consuming. Many of the problems could be directly linked to the behaviour of managers, as the interviews with employees revealed.

These problems of appraisals and the role of line managers in conducting them were anticipated some time ago by Grint (3). He concluded that 'rarely in the history of business can such a system have promised so much and delivered so little'. And he suggested that appraisals are unlikely to bear a close or, indeed, any relationship to reality because of the impossibility of 'being able to reduce the complex nature of any individual to a series of scales in a check list', and the remote possibility 'of ever achieving objective appraisals of a subordinate by a superior'. This 'radical critique' of performance appraisal is one shared by many academics as well as those referred to above (see also Chapter 5 of *Performance Management: The new realities*, Armstrong and Baron, 4). Performance appraisal has been and still is an easy target, shot at by practitioners as well as academics (Armstrong and Murlis, 5, refer to it as often being 'a dishonest annual ritual'). What needs to be done is to decide how to overcome these objections. Overall, this is a matter of adopting a performance management approach as described in this book (the differences between performance management and performance appraisal were discussed in Chapter 1, pages 9–10). Specifically it means addressing the issues of implementing performance management effectively.

Addressing the issues

These issues are more likely to arise in an old-fashioned performance appraisal system, which involves ratings and, often, a direct and formulaic link to performance-related pay. But they can also occur in more up-to-date performance management processes, which even if they emphasize dialogue and agreement rather than control from above still depend on the commitment and ability of line managers to carry out the process in a way that will meet the needs of all the stakeholders – the organization, the manager and, importantly, the individual.

It is relatively easy to design a performance management 'system'; it is much more difficult to make it work. There are no quick fixes. But it is important to ensure that all the stakeholders are involved in the development of the system (see Chapter 14) and that all concerned are given as much opportunity as possible to learn about performance management, through communications, formal training and, best of all, especially for line managers, less formal ways of helping people to learn the demanding skills involved such as coaching and mentoring (see Chapter 15). It is necessary to gain the commitment of line managers and also ensure that they are capable of carrying out their performance management responsibilities.

Gaining the commitment of line managers

Too often, line managers regard performance management in the shape of the formal review as a bureaucratic chore. They believe, rightly or wrongly, that they are doing it anyway, so they say 'Why should we conform to a system imposed on us by the HR department?' Even if they don't believe that formal reviews are a waste of time, some managers are reluctant to conduct them because they find it difficult to criticize people and imagine that they will be faced by unpleasant confrontations. Others are nervous about reviews because they feel that they lack the skills required to provide feedback, analyse performance and agree objectives.

Gaining the commitment of line managers takes a lot of time, effort and persistence but it has to be done. Here are some of the approaches that can be used.

Provide leadership from the top

As mentioned earlier in this chapter, top management has a crucial role to play in implementing performance management. They have to communicate and act on the belief that performance management is an integral part of the fabric of the managerial practices of the organization. They should demonstrate their conviction that this is what good management is about and this is how managers are expected to play their part.

Communicate

Simply telling line managers that performance management is a good thing will not get you very far. But somehow the message has to reach them that managing performance is what managers are expected to do. The message should come from the top and be cascaded down through the organization. It should not come from HR except, incidentally, as part of a training or induction programme. The message should be built into management development programmes, especially for potential managers. It should be understood by them from the outset that performance management is an important part of their responsibilities and that these are the skills they must acquire and use. The significance of performance management can also be conveyed by including the effectiveness with which managers carry out their performance management responsibilities as one of the criteria used when assessing their performance.

Keep it simple

Willing participation in performance management activities is more likely to be achieved if managers do not see it as a bureaucratic chore. If forms are used – and they don't have to be – they should be as simple as possible, no more than two sides of one piece of paper. It should be emphasized that performance management is not a form-filling exercise and that the important thing is the dialogue between managers and individuals that continues throughout the year and is not just an annual event.

Reduce the pressure

Line managers can feel pressurized and exposed if they perceive that performance management is just about carrying out an annual appraisal meeting in which they have to tell employees where they have gone wrong, rate their performance and decide on the pay increase they should be given. This pressure can be reduced if the emphasis is on 'performance management throughout the year'. It should not be treated as an annual event. Rather, it should be regarded as part of normal good management practice, which involves recognizing good work as it happens, dealing with performance problems as they arise and revising roles and objectives as required. The annual review meeting takes the form of a stock-taking exercise – no surprises

– but, more importantly, becomes a forward-looking exercise – where do we go from here?

Pressure can also be reduced if managers do not have to make and defend ratings, although they still have to reach agreement on areas for development and improvement and what needs to be done about them. A further reduction of pressure can be achieved if pay reviews are 'decoupled' from performance reviews, ie they take place several months later.

Involve

Involve line managers in the design and development of performance management processes as members of project teams or by taking part in pilot studies. This could be extended by the use of focus groups and general surveys of opinions and reactions. They can also be involved in reviewing the effectiveness of performance management. Commitment can be enhanced by getting line managers to act as coaches in developing performance management skills and as mentors to managers unfamiliar with the process. The more performance management is owned by line managers the better.

Encourage

Line managers can be encouraged to believe in performance management through communities of practice – gatherings of managers during which information is exchanged on good practice. They are more likely to take notice of their peers than someone from HR. But HR can still play a useful role in encouraging managers.

Developing capability and improving performance

Clearly, systematic formal training as described in Chapter 15 is necessary in the performance management skills managers need to use. This should take place when launching a new scheme but, importantly, also during management development programmes for potential managers and induction programmes for new managers. Coaching and guidance to individual managers should be provided to supplement formal training. This can be provided by HR specialists although, better still, experienced, committed and competent line managers can be used as coaches and mentors.

It is also necessary to monitor the performance of managers as performance managers. This is not just a matter of checking on completed performance management forms as practised in some organizations.

However, HR specialists or, preferably, line manager mentors can usefully follow up newly appointed or promoted managers to discuss how they are getting on and provide advice on dealing with any problems. 360-degree feedback or upward assessment can be used to review the performance management abilities of line managers when dealing with their staff and to indicate on an individual basis where improvements are required. Regular surveys can be conducted of the reactions of employees to performance management, which can lead to the identification of any common weaknesses and the remedial action required.

THE ROLE OF EMPLOYEES

Every employee, from the top to the bottom of an organization, is subject to performance management even if this is not necessarily a formal process. Their pay and future is affected by it and in the more formal schemes they take part in formulating performance agreements and measuring and reviewing performance. They may be asked to prepare for review meetings formally or take part in 360-degree assessment schemes. They will participate in objective setting and discussing roles and competence requirements. They need to be briefed and, often, trained in all these activities.

THE ROLE OF HR

At one time, the personnel department tended to be the sponsor and custodian of performance appraisal schemes. As a result, line managers regarded them as the preserve of personnel and therefore not their concern. They filled up the forms, often because they had to, but unenthusiastically. The emergence of the 'business partner' concept of HR led to a change in direction. HR no longer ran the performance appraisal scheme; instead their role became that of encouraging and facilitating the sort of performance management processes described earlier in this book. They work alongside line managers, helping them as necessary to develop their skills and encouraging their use. Importantly, they assemble teams of committed and experienced managers who can act as coaches and mentors and stimulate the creation of communities of practice, ensuring that performance management is on the agenda. More specifically, they run training events and conduct surveys to evaluate the effectiveness of performance management. In essence, HR specialists exist to support performance management rather than drive it.

REFERENCES

1 Purcell, J et al (2003) Understanding the People and Performance Link: Unlocking the black box, CIPD, London
2 Hutchinson, S and Purcell, J (2003) Bringing Policies to Life: The vital role of front line managers in people management, CIPD, London
3 Grint, K (1993) What's wrong with performance appraisal? A critique and a suggestion, Human Resource Management Journal, Spring, pp 61–77
4 Armstong, M and Baron, A (1998) Performance Management: The new realities, Institute of Personnel and Development, London
5 Armstrong, M and Murlis, H (1998) Reward Management, 4th edn, Kogan Page, London

14

Introducing and developing performance management

APPROACH TO DEVELOPMENT

Excellent practical advice on introducing performance management or making substantial changes to an existing scheme was given by the respondents to the e-reward 2005 survey (1) – see Chapter 3. This is summarized below with quotations from respondents to illustrate their views.

Dos

The most frequently mentioned 'dos' in order of frequency were:

- Consult/involve.
- Provide training.
- Communicate (process and benefits).
- Get buy-in from senior management.
- Align and ensure relevance to organizational/business/stakeholder needs.

▌ Keep it simple.

▌ Get ownership from line managers.

▌ Ensure clear purpose and processes.

▌ Monitor and evaluate.

▌ Align to culture.

▌ Plan and prepare carefully.

▌ Align with other HR processes.

▌ Run a pilot scheme.

▌ Clarify link to reward.

▌ Treat as a business process.

▌ Be realistic about the scale and pace of change.

▌ Define performance expectations.

▌ Make process mandatory.

Examples of comments

▌ 'Get buy-in from senior management from the start.'

▌ 'Keep it simple. Keep it transparent. Train, train, train!'

▌ 'You can never do enough training/coaching of both staff and line managers. You can never do too little communication on the new changes.'

▌ 'Ensure the process is seen as a business one not an HR process.'

▌ 'Keep it simple and concentrate on the quality going into the process rather than the design of the process itself (although the design must be appropriate to the organization).'

▌ 'Ensure that there is an understanding in the line of how the process can help the business – so it's not seen as an "HR add-on" process. Get buy-in from senior management from the start. Involve staff in development. Keep it simple. Train, train, train managers. Review effectiveness.'

▌ 'Engage all managers in why it is important and ensure that they have the necessary understanding and skills to carry out the process. Get buy-in and tailor it to the specific needs of the organization. Get the support of key stakeholders such as the union from the start, and get them to work with you to sell the scheme. Agree the overall objectives and guiding principles with all concerned. Keep employees informed and ensure the message is consistent throughout.'

▌ 'Aim to maintain clarity throughout the process and construct transparent support documentation for the users. Use a group of people to run your ideas through and give feedback to make sure you are achieving what you set out to achieve.'

▌ 'Consider the desired output in terms of results and behaviours you want the system to achieve. Consider the training requirements for the managers and staff expected to use the system. Spend sufficient time on communication and change management. Bear in mind that the more complex the scheme, the less transparent it may become and the more time it may take to administer!'

▌ 'Do involve managers and staff in the development of the process through focus groups and take on board their input. Develop a comprehensive communications programme adjusted in style for different populations. Ensure appropriate training has taken place before launching. Track the implementation to analyse success. Include completing performance management/reviews in managers'/supervisors' objectives so that part of their performance review is based on this criterion.'

▌ 'Understand clearly why you are doing it and the desired objectives. Engage others in design of scheme. Communicate purpose etc clearly. Get line managers/supervisors on board. Train all. Consider how you will evaluate success.'

Don'ts

The most common 'don'ts' in order of frequency were:

▌ Don't just make it a form-filling, paper-intensive exercise.

▌ Don't make it too complicated.

▌ Don't rush in a new system.

▌ Don't underestimate the time it takes to introduce.   .

▌ Don't keep changing the system.

▌ Don't assume managers have the skills required.

- Don't link to pay.
- Don't blindly follow others.
- Don't neglect communication, consultation and training.
- Don't assume that everyone wants it.

Examples of comments

- 'Don't expect that staff will leap for joy at the prospect of another way they would see of criticizing them in their job. Start your change management process where you think the staff are, not where you've assumed they are.'

- 'Don't assume that what seems obvious and logical to you, as an HR manager, will also seem logical to other managers and staff. Don't get caught up in HR speak and become precious about the differences between "performance management" and "appraisals" or between a "personal development/learning plan" and a "training plan". As HR professionals we may be able to eloquently argue the subtle differences and merits of each – for most people the distinction is absolutely meaningless!'

- 'Don't just make it a form-filling exercise – you need to gain the belief from managers that the system is beneficial; otherwise it won't work.'

- 'Don't put in a lengthy, complicated process – it will become a chore to do rather than a meaningful exercise.'

- 'Don't make HR own the initiative – it is a business improvement model and one which the business needs to manage.'

- 'Don't implement without investigating main needs and requirements, implement without sufficient training for managers, try to aim too high at the start.'

- 'Don't assume that supervisors have the requisite skills to manage performance fairly and equitably, embark upon such an initiative without clear goals and without the support of respected key players in the organization, set the wheels in motion until extensive briefings/training have been completed.'

- 'Don't underestimate the amount of work involved!'

▮ 'Don't underestimate the time it takes to embed, underestimate how managers wriggle to avoid making judgements, meet with unions until you are sure of where you intend to head, and the costs are approved.'

▮ 'Don't expect it to work quickly. It takes a few years to embed performance management in the organization's ethos.'

THE DEVELOPMENT FRAMEWORK

Performance management can be regarded as a framework, as illustrated in Figure 14.1, within which a number of factors operate that will affect how it should be developed, introduced and evaluated.

The framework or essence of performance management is provided by the arrangements for agreeing performance requirements or expectations, preparing performance plans, managing performance throughout the year and reviewing performance.

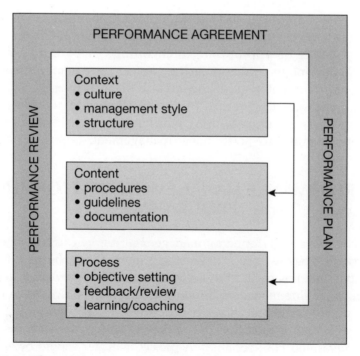

Figure 14.1 The performance development framework

CONTEXTUAL FACTORS

Inside this framework are the contextual or environmental factors of culture, management style and structure, which will strongly influence the content of performance management procedures, guidelines and documentation and the all-important processes that make it work (objective setting, attribute and competence analysis, providing feedback, counselling and coaching).

Cultural considerations will affect performance management because it works best when it fits the existing values of the organization. Ideally, these should support high performance, quality, involvement, openness, freedom of communication and mutual trust. These may not have been put into practice in full, however vigorously they have been espoused. But top management must genuinely want to move in these directions and need to make it clear that everyone else should go along with them, using performance management as a lever for change. In performance management, there is too often a gap between the rhetoric and the reality. The process of developing and introducing performance management must concentrate on ensuring that worthy ambitions are translated into effective action by all concerned.

Structural considerations will also affect the way in which performance management is introduced. In a highly decentralized organization, or one in which considerable authority and power are devolved to some functions or divisions, it may be appropriate to encourage or permit each unit or function to develop its own approach to performance management as long as they conform to central guidelines on its basic principles.

The cultural and structural factors to be taken into account will vary considerably between organizations, which is why there is no one best way to develop and introduce performance management.

PERFORMANCE MANAGEMENT DEVELOPMENT PROGRAMME

The development of performance management can be carried out in the 10 stages described below. At each stage arrangements should be made to consult and involve staff. It is particularly important to make every effort to gain the commitment of line managers through involvement (in order to promote ownership) and communications. It is desirable to set up a project team to develop performance management composed of managers, staff, trade union representatives and HR specialists. A project manager should be appointed who, together with the project team, should report to a steering committee of senior managers.

Stage 1: Decide on the business case for introducing performance management

The business case for introducing performance management should be agreed by top management. Essentially, this could be to develop a high-performance culture in order to achieve business goals by improving the performance of individuals and teams and ensuring that individual objectives are integrated with corporate objectives.

Stage 2: Determine objectives and guiding principles for performance management

Performance management must be designed to meet business needs. Specific objectives could include:

▮ to improve organizational, team and individual performance;

▮ to provide for the closer integration of organizational, team and individual objectives and thus focus people on doing the right things;

▮ to clarify expectations on what individuals and teams have to achieve;

▮ to support the realization of the organization's core values;

▮ to develop individuals' skills and capabilities;

▮ to foster a closer relationship between individuals and their managers based on the agreement of objectives, feedback and coaching;

▮ to provide for a more objective and fairer method of assessing performance;

▮ to empower individuals to manage their own performance and learning.

Stage 3: Get the commitment and active participation of top management and line managers

The power of the words and behaviour of top managers should never be underestimated. They can set the example and build commitment at all levels. They need to be convinced that there is a powerful business case for performance management. Once they are on side, get them actively engaged as champions for performance management.

It is equally important to develop the engagement of line managers. It is they who will implement performance management and if they are not on board the system will probably fail.

Stage 4: Draw up guiding principles on how performance management should work

The guiding principles should emphasize that performance management is regarded as a normal and continuous process of management that is owned by the managers and staff who are involved. It should be made clear that it operates as a partnership between managers and their staff who are equally involved in planning and reviewing performance and in implementing personal development and performance improvement plans.

The following is an example of guiding principles developed by a working party in a local authority:

▌ clearly stated work objectives/tasks subject to regular review and updating;

▌ clearly stated standards of performance;

▌ feedback on job behaviour;

▌ comments rather than performance ratings;

▌ identification of development needs;

▌ agreed training plan;

▌ reach agreement through a two-way process;

▌ incorporate appeal procedure;

▌ used as a day-to-day management tool;

▌ no link to pay;

▌ if no commitment from the head of department, don't do it.

Stage 5: Define performance management processes and documentation

Each stage of the performance management cycle needs to be defined. The performance agreement and planning process are first. It is necessary to define how role profiles should be agreed and used as the basis for performance management, how objectives and targets should be set, how performance measures should be agreed, and how performance improvement and personal development plans should be drawn up. Secondly, the basis upon which performance management should be a continuous process (performance management throughout the year) through informal reviews of progress and feedback should be explained. Finally, the approach to conducting performance reviews should be explained. Rating methods, if required, have to be decided and thought given to how to ensure that they are consistent and fair. The link, if any, between performance management and performance or contribution pay also needs to be determined.

Documentation should be drawn up at this stage with guidelines on how it should be used. The watchword is 'keep it simple'. Complex and lengthy forms are a major cause of performance management failure. It should be emphasized that the forms should simply act as an aide-memoire. They should not be allowed to dominate the procedure.

Stage 6: Pilot-test

It is essential to pilot-test performance management in two or three different types of departments. The procedures as set out on paper must be exposed to real-life conditions so that problems and issues in applying them can be identified. The tests will indicate what changes need to be made but they will also reveal what managers and staff have to learn about performance management and thus feed into the implementation programme during which steps are taken to ensure that everyone learns what they need to know. If the departments are selected carefully with a committed management team and staff who are likely to be cooperative, the pilot test can identify champions of performance management who can act as coaches and mentors and provide practical guidance.

The test should cover the main performance management processes, ie developing role profiles, setting objectives, deciding on performance measures, formulating performance improvement and development plans, conducting performance reviews, giving feedback and coaching, and completing the documentation. Ideally, it should cover the whole 12-month cycle. This may be too long but at least three months and preferably six should be allowed. Superficial tests are worse than useless. Performance management takes time to establish. It should never be rushed.

Stage 7: Communicate

Considerable care needs to be taken to communicate to all concerned – managers, team leaders, staff and trade union representatives – the aims of performance management, how it will work and how people will be affected by it. The communication strategy should have been a constant preoccupation of the developers of the scheme. They should consider for each feature of the process as it is being developed how it can be explained and presented to the people concerned.

Communication can be through documentation (an explanatory brochure), the intranet and face-to-face briefings (the more of the latter the better). The following is an example of a guide to performance management prepared by a not-for-profit organization:

A GUIDE TO PERFORMANCE MANAGEMENT

Introduction

The purpose of performance management is to help and encourage everyone to raise their performance, develop their abilities, increase job satisfaction and achieve their full potential to the benefit of the individual and the organization as a whole.

What is performance management?

Performance management is a means of getting better results from the organization, teams and individuals by understanding and managing performance within an agreed framework of planned goals, and standards.

It is based on the simple proposition that when people know and understand what is expected of them, and have been able to take part in forming those expectations, they can and will meet them.

Why do we need performance management?

There are two main reasons for introducing performance management:

1. We want to focus everyone's attention on what they are expected to achieve in their jobs and how best to achieve it.

2. We would like to help everyone to identify and satisfy their development needs – to improve performance and realize their potential.

How does performance management work?

Performance management works like this:

▌ You and your manager will discuss and agree your objectives, action plans and development and training needs – this is called the performance agreement.

▌ During the review period (normally 12 months) you and your manager will keep under review your progress in meeting your objectives – as necessary you will agree revisions to those objectives and your priorities.

▌ Towards the end of the review period you and your manager will separately prepare for the performance and development review meeting – deciding in advance on any points you wish to raise and noting these down on a preparation form.

▌ A review meeting will then be held at which you can discuss with your manager how you got on during the review period and any other points you want to raise. You will then together draw up a new performance agreement.

▌ Your manager's manager will see the form and will add any comments he or she feels may be appropriate. You will also see these comments.

▌ You and your manager will then retain your own copies of the review form – no other copies will be held by anyone else.

Performance management will:

▌ focus on developing strengths as well as considering any performance problems;

▌ be based on open and constructive discussion;

▌ be an everyday and natural management process – not an annual form-filling exercise;

▌ be a positive process – looking to the future rather than dwelling on the past.

The part you will play

We hope that you will contribute to the success of this scheme in the following ways:

▌ by preparing carefully for the review – noting any points you want to raise with your manager;

▌ by entering into the spirit of the review meeting, which is intended to provide an opportunity for you to have 'quality time' with your manager during which an open and friendly exchange of views will take place about your job and your prospects;

▌ by thinking carefully about how you are going to achieve the objectives and plans agreed at the meeting;

▌ by reviewing how you are getting on during the year and agreeing any actions required.

The part managers will play

All managers will be expected to play their part with you in preparing for the meeting, reviewing your performance and drawing up your performance agreement. They are being specially trained in how to do this. Managers are also expected to work with you in preparing and implementing your personal development plan.

Benefits to you

We hope performance management will benefit you by ensuring that:

▌ you know what is expected of you;

▌ you know how you stand;

▌ you know what you need to do to reach your objectives;

▌ you can discuss with your manager your present job, your development and training needs and your future.

Benefits to your manager

Managers will gain the opportunity to:

▌ clarify expectations with the individual members of their teams;

▌ have 'quality time' with their staff to discuss matters affecting work, performance and development away from the hurly-burly of everyday working life;

▌ provide better feedback to individuals about their performance and progress based on a mutual understanding of needs;

▌ identify areas of individual concern and provide guidance to enable individuals to make the best use of their abilities;

▌ build closer working relationships based on mutual trust and respect;

▌ identify individual training and development needs.

Benefits to the organization

The organization gains the opportunity to:

▌ integrate individual, team and corporate objectives;

▌ guide individual and team effort to meeting overall business needs;

▌ recognize individual contribution;

▌ plan individual careers;

▌ introduce relevant and effective learning and development programmes to meet identified needs.

The benefits of performance management for staff were defined by a major union as follows:

The Personal Development Review System gives us all a better understanding of:

▌ our role and contribution to the success of the Union;

▌ what we are trying to achieve;

▌ how we will achieve our plans;

▌ how we will be able to evaluate our performance;

▌ our development needs;

▌ how our performance will be assessed.

We all benefit by:

▌ being valued;

▌ developing our skills;

▌ achieving our goals.

The Union benefits by:

▌ having a clearly defined means of translating business and strategic plans into action;

▌ staff commitment and motivation;

▌ flexibility;

▌ good communication;

▌ high standards of performance from members of staff.

A local authority described the benefits of its performance management system as follows:

▌ Clear direction on what is expected and what you need to do to achieve your objectives.

- Regular supervision and support from your manager.

- An annual appraisal.

- Discussion about your development and, if you are interested, an opportunity to review your career development.

- Recognition of the contribution you make and its importance to the service.

- An opportunity to influence your team's work plan as well as your future work.

Stage 8: Plan arrangements for training in performance management

It is essential to provide training for both line managers and staff generally in performance management. It is particularly important that line managers have the skills required. These are demanding and the programme should provide for coaching, mentoring and ongoing guidance as well as formal training courses. A half- or one-day course, which is the typical time the e-reward research established was devoted to training, is not enough. Training arrangements are described in Chapter 15.

Stage 9: Implement

The implementation programme should cover communications, training and the provision of guidance and help.

Stage 10: Evaluate

It is important to carry out a thorough evaluation as described in Chapter 16 of how performance management works after its first year of operation.

REFERENCES

1   e-reward (2005) *Survey of Performance Management Practice*, e-reward, Stockport

15

Learning about performance management

To introduce and sustain performance management successfully it is essential to ensure that all concerned – individuals as well as managers – learn about how performance management works and why it is important, and develop the skills they need. The objectives of a performance management learning programme are to:

▌ let people know about the rationale for the processes with which they will be involved – these will include the business drivers that have led the organization to introduce performance management as well as a description of the processes themselves;

▌ spell out their contribution – why it is important, how they make it and the benefits that will accrue to them and the organization;

▌ develop the skills people have to use.

THE RATIONALE FOR PERFORMANCE MANAGEMENT

Performance management may be regarded with indifference ('it doesn't concern me'), suspicion ('a waste of time'), cynicism ('we've seen it all before') or outright hostility ('it won't work'). These negative reactions must be overcome by leadership from the top, communications (oral briefings as well as the intranet and brochures), training, coaching and mentoring.

It is vital to get the message across that top management regards the process as a vital part of the drive to improve performance. A business case for performance management must be made by demonstrating how it will contribute to improving organizational effectiveness and overall performance. It should be treated as a crucial component in the drive to develop a high-performance culture. The message should be delivered as strongly as possible that performance management is about how performance is managed in the organization – a core value. It should be treated as a normal process of management, which is owned by line managers, not the HR department.

CONTRIBUTION

It is important to reinforce the messages about the business case for performance management with more precise information on the parts played by managers and individuals. The emphasis should be on the need for partnership and dialogue, the open and honest exchange of information (feedback) and sharing the process to the mutual benefit of both parties.

When spelling out the contribution of managers and team leaders the message should be that they are there to help and to coach, not to judge. For individuals, the message will be how they can benefit from self-assessment and the part they can play in developing themselves.

SKILLS

Performance management is not easy. It requires high levels of skill by everyone involved, and the skills are likely to be ones that have not yet been developed or put into practice. For example, providing feedback that will motivate and help to develop people is not easy to those who have not done it before. Receiving, responding to and acting on feedback are similarly unfamiliar skills for many people. The agreement of objectives and competence requirements, the application of performance measures and methods of analysing and using the outcomes of reviews may also be strange. The concepts of personal development planning and self-managed learning will be new to many people.

The main performance management skills that people need to learn are:

- preparing role profiles – defining key result areas and competence requirements;

- defining objectives;

- identifying and using performance measures;

- giving and receiving feedback;

- taking part in review meetings – ensuring that there is a proper dialogue that enables the manager and the individual jointly, frankly and freely to discuss performance requirements and learning needs;

- identifying learning needs and preparing and implementing personal development plans;

- diagnosing and solving performance problems;

- coaching.

FORMAL LEARNING

All these skills should be covered in a performance management learning programme, which can take the form of modules dealing with the overall processes and skills. An example of a programme on reviewing performance is given below:

Workshop aims

On completing this workshop participants will:

- understand the purpose of performance reviews;

- know how to prepare for a constructive review;

- know how to conduct an effective performance review;

- be able to provide good feedback;

- have gained some initial understanding of the processes of coaching and counselling.

Programme

9.00   Objectives of the workshop

9.30   The purpose of the performance review

10.00	Preparing for the review
10.30	Coffee
10.45	Giving feedback
11.15	Conducting the review
12.30	Lunch
13.30	Practice in conducting reviews (1)
15.00	Tea
15.15	Practice in conducting reviews (2)
16.30	Putting the review to good use
17.00	Close

Methods

Learning, especially skills development, should be achieved by participative methods – guided discussions, role plays and other exercises.

Guided discussion

The aim of guided discussions is to get participants to think through for themselves the learning points. When covering review meetings the trainer asks questions such as:

▊ What do you think makes for a good review meeting? Can you provide any example from your previous experience?

▊ What do you think can go wrong with a meeting? Have you any examples?

▊ Why is it important to create the right environment?

▊ How do you set about doing so?

▊ What sort of things should be discussed in a review meeting?

▊ Why is it important for managers to let the individual do most of the talking?

▊ Why could self-assessment be useful?

Role plays

Role plays are usually based on a written brief, which defines the same situation from each participant's point of view so that participants can understand what it feels like to be in either position.

Course members are then asked to play out the roles and fellow members assess their performance (this in itself provides some practice in performance assessment). Each person playing the role will also describe his or her feelings about the review, and assess the other person's performance or behaviour.

Exercises

An approach that can be more realistic is to get participants to perform a task on which they are appraised by fellow course members. This could be a group exercise. If there is sufficient time available each member could take it in turn to lead the group and be appraised on their performance by the rest of the group. Such exercises can also be used to practise formulating team objectives and reviewing team performance.

A further variation is to get one course member to give a short presentation on a topic, have a second one assess the presenter and get a third person to assess the quality of the assessment. This gives the opportunity to practise assessment skills.

LESS FORMAL LEARNING

Formal training programmes are useful but not enough. Performance management skills are best developed through coaching and mentoring. The HR department can play an important role in organizing these learning activities but it is best to use experienced line managers as coaches and mentors.

16

Evaluating performance management

It is clearly important to monitor the introduction of performance management very carefully but it is equally vital to continue to monitor and evaluate it regularly, especially after its first year of operation.

METHOD

The best method of monitoring and evaluation is to ask those involved – managers and individuals – how it worked. As many as possible should be seen, individually and in groups, to discuss the points set out in the 'Points to be covered' section of this chapter. The evaluation can be carried out by members of a project team and/or by the HR function.

Individual interviews and focus group discussions can be supplemented by a special survey of reactions to performance management, which could be completed anonymously by all managers and staff. The results should be fed back to all concerned and analysed to assess the need for any amendments to the process or further training requirements. An example of a performance review evaluation form and typical attitude survey questions are given in Figures 16.1 and 16.2.

1   How effectively was the review meeting conducted in each of the areas listed below?

Rate each aspect of the review meeting as follows:

1   =   very effectively
2   =   effectively
3   =   fairly effectively
4   =   not very effectively

creating and maintaining an informal and friendly atmosphere	
working to a clear structure	
keeping control of the meeting	
using praise	
handling criticism	
letting the individual do most of the talking	
inviting self-assessment	
focusing on facts – discussing performance not personality	
agreeing a plan of action	

2   How would you rate the overall effectiveness of the meeting:

▮ very effective
▮ effective
▮ fairly effective
▮ ineffective

3   How did you feel after the meeting:

▮ highly motivated
▮ reasonably well motivated
▮ not very well motivated
▮ demotivated

4   Comments – reasons for the ratings given above

Figure 16.1   Performance review evaluation form

Please indicate how you felt about performance management by recording your reactions to the following statements. Indicate:

A = If you fully agree

B = If you partly agree

C = If you disagree

1. I am quite satisfied that the objectives I agreed were fair.
2. I felt that the meeting to agree objectives and standards of performance helped me to focus on what I should be aiming to achieve.
3. I received good feedback from my manager on how I was doing.
4. My manager was always prepared to provide guidance when I ran into problems at work.
5. The performance review meeting was conducted by my manager in a friendly and helpful way.
6. My manager fully recognized my achievements during the year.
7. If any criticisms were made during the review meeting, they were acceptable because they were based on fact, not opinion.
8. I was given plenty of opportunity by my manager to discuss the reasons for any of my work problems.
9. I felt generally that the comments made by my manager at the meeting were fair.
10. The meeting ended with a clear plan of action for the future with which I agreed.
11. I felt motivated after the meeting.
12. I felt that the time spent in the meeting was well worthwhile.

Figure 16.2 Performance management attitude survey questionnaire

The ultimate test, of course, is analysing organizational performance to establish the extent to which improvements can be attributed to performance management. It may be difficult to establish a direct connection but more detailed assessments with managers and staff on the impact of the process may reveal specific areas in which performance has been improved, which could be linked to an overall performance measure.

A TYPICAL APPROACH

When performance management was introduced in an NHS trust it was decided that monitoring could be carried out by:

▌ recording and analysing performance assessments, which helps establish how managers are using performance management;

▍ one-to-one interviews with managers, identifying how they are finding the experience of performance management and where they need more support;

▍ employee attitude surveys and focused discussion groups;

▍ reviewing improvements in the performance of the organization.

To maintain high standards it was deemed necessary to:

▍ maintain training in performance management for all new staff (including individuals who were promoted to management posts);

▍ top up training to keep the principles and practices fresh;

▍ use one-to-one coaching where necessary;

▍ conduct workshops for managers to share their experiences.

These guidelines are valid for any organization that wants to develop and maintain effective performance management processes.

POINTS TO BE COVERED

The questions that should be answered in an evaluation of performance management are:

Performance agreements

1. Are performance agreements being completed properly?
2. Do they generally spell out realistic objectives, attribute and competence requirements, work plans and performance improvement and development plans?

Objectives

3. Are objectives being agreed properly?
4. Are they related clearly to key result areas?
5. Do they generally meet agreed criteria for good objectives, ie are they demanding but attainable, relevant, measurable, agreed and time based?
6. Are they integrated with organizational and departmental objectives?

7. Are individuals and teams given scope to contribute to the formulation of higher-level objectives?

Performance standards

8. Are performance standards agreed for key aspects of the job where time-based and quantifiable objectives cannot be set?

Performance measures

9. Are appropriate performance measures being agreed?

Feedback

10. Are managers providing good feedback throughout the year as well as during formal review meetings?

Performance reviews

11. Are both managers and individuals preparing properly for performance review meetings?

12. How well are managers conducting such meetings, with particular reference to:
    - creating the right (informal) atmosphere;
    - working to a clear structure;
    - using praise to get people to relax, to motivate and to provide them with encouragement;
    - letting the individual do most of the talking;
    - inviting self-appraisal;
    - discussing performance not personality;
    - being positive – facing up to situations;
    - not springing surprises on the individuals they are assessing;
    - agreeing realistic and measurable objectives and a plan of action.

Motivation

13. How effective has performance management been in motivating employees?

Development

14. How effective has performance management been in developing skills and capabilities?

15. How well have managers and team leaders carried out their role as coach, counsellor and mentor?

Ratings

16. Have ratings been fair and consistently applied?

Performance-related pay

17. Do managers and employees feel that rewards under the performance-related pay scheme are properly and fairly linked to their performance?

18. How well do they think that performance-related pay is acting as a motivator?

Documentation

19. How well have the performance management forms been completed?

Briefing and training

20. How effective have the briefing and training programmes been?

OUTCOME

The outcome of the evaluation should be a report that summarizes findings and indicates what actions are required to correct shortcomings in the shape of change to the arrangements and/or further briefing and training.

References

Armstrong, M (1976) *A Handbook of Personnel Management Practice*, Kogan Page, London

Armstrong, M and Baron, A (1998) *Performance Management: The new realities*, Institute of Personnel and Development, London

Armstrong, M and Baron, A (2004) *Managing Performance: Performance management in action*, CIPD, London

Armstrong, M and Murlis, H (1994) *Reward Management*, Kogan Page, London

Armstrong, M and Murlis, H (1998) *Reward Management*, 4th edn, Kogan Page, London

Beer, M and Ruh, R A (1976) Employee growth through performance management, *Harvard Business Review*, July–August, pp 59–66

Brumbach, G B (1988) Some ideas, issues and predictions about performance management, *Public Personnel Management*, Winter, pp 387–402

Deming, W E (1986) *Out of the Crisis*, MIT Centre for Advanced Engineering Studies, Cambridge, MA

Egan, G (1995) A clear path to peak performance, *People Management*, 18 May, pp 34–37

e-reward (2004) *Report on Contingent Pay*, e-reward, Stockport

e-reward (2005) *Survey of Performance Management Practice*, e-reward, Stockport

Fletcher, C (1993) *Appraisal: Routes to improved performance*, Institute of Personnel and Development, London

Grint, K (1993) What's wrong with performance appraisal? A critique and a suggestion, *Human Resource Management Journal*, Spring, pp 61–77

Guest, D E *et al* (1996) *The State of the Psychological Contract in Employment*, Institute of Personnel and Development, London

Handy, C (1989) *The Age of Unreason*, Business Books, London

Handy, L, Devine, M and Heath, L (1996) *360-Degree Feedback: Unguided missile or powerful weapon?*, Ashridge Management Group, Berkhamsted

Hutchinson, S and Purcell, J (2003) *Bringing Policies to Life: The vital role of front line managers in people management*, CIPD, London

IRS Employment Review (2003) Performance management: policy and practice, August, pp 12–19

Kaplan, R S and Norton, D P (1992) The balanced scorecard – measures that drive performance, *Harvard Business Review*, January–February, pp 71–79

Kessler, I and Purcell, J (1993) *The Templeton Performance-Related Pay Project: Summary of key findings*, Templeton College, Oxford

Lawler, E E and McDermott, M (2003) Current performance management practices, *WorldatWork Journal*, Second quarter, pp 49–60

Levinson, H (1970) Management by whose objectives?, *Harvard Business Review*, July–August, pp 125–34

Lockett, J (1992) *Effective Performance Management*, Kogan Page, London

London, M and Beatty, R W (1993) 360-degree feedback as competitive advantage, *Human Resource Management*, Summer/Fall, pp 353–72

McGregor, D (1957) An uneasy look at performance appraisal, *Harvard Business Review*, May–June, pp 89–94

Maier, N (1958) *The Appraisal Interview*, Wiley, New York

Mohrman, A M and Mohrman, S A (1995) Performance management is 'running the business', *Compensation and Benefits Review*, July–August, pp 69–75

O'Malley, M (2003) Forced ranking, *WorldatWork Journal*, First quarter, pp 31–39

Purcell, J *et al* (2003) *Understanding the People and Performance Link: Unlocking the black box*, CIPD, London

Reynolds, J (2004) *Helping People Learn*, CIPD, London

Risher, H (2003) Refocusing performance management for high performance, *Compensation and Benefits Review*, September–October, pp 20–30

Rothwell, W (2002) *Models for Human Resource Improvement*, 2nd edn, American Society for Training and Development, Alexandria, VA

Rousseau, D M (1988) The construction of climate in organizational research, in *International Review of Industrial and Organizational Psychology*, ed L C Cooper and I Robertson, Wiley, Chichester

Rowe, K H (1964) An appraisal of appraisals, *Journal of Management Studies*, **1** (1), March, pp 1–25

Schaffer, R H (1991) Demand better results and get them, *Harvard Business Review*, March–April, pp 142–49

Sloman, M (2003) *Training in the Age of the Learner*, CIPD, London

Turnow, W W (1993) Introduction to special issues on 360-degree feedback, *Human Resource Management*, Summer/Fall, pp 311–16

Walters, M (1995) *The Performance Management Handbook*, Institute of Personnel and Development, London

Ward, P (1997) *360-Degree Feedback*, Institute of Personnel and Development, London

Winstanley, D and Stuart-Smith, K (1996) Policing performance: the ethics of performance management, *Personnel Review*, **25** (6), pp 66–84

Further reading

Advisory, Conciliation and Arbitration Service (1988) *Employee Appraisal*, ACAS, London

Antonioni, D (1994) Improve the performance management process before discontinuing performance appraisals, *Compensation and Benefits Review*, May–June, pp 29–37

Baguley, P (1994) *Improving Organisational Performance*, McGraw-Hill, Maidenhead

Bailey, R T (1983) *Measurement of Performance*, Gower, Aldershot

Barlow, G (1989) Deficiencies and the perpetuation of power: latent functions in performance appraisal, *Journal of Management Studies*, September, pp 499–517

Baron, A and Armstrong, M (2004) Get into line, *People Management*, 14 October, pp 44–46

Bates, R A and Holton, E F (1995) Computerised performance monitoring: a review of human resource issues, *Human Resource Management Review*, Winter, pp 267–88

Bates, S (2003) Forced ranking, *HR Magazine*, June, pp 65–68

Beaver, G and Harris, L (1995) Performance management and the small firm: dilemmas, tensions and paradoxes, *Journal of Strategic Change*, **4**, pp 109–19

Bernadin, H K *et al* (1995) Performance appraisal design, development and implementation, in G R Ferris, S D Rosen and D J Barnum (eds), *Handbook of Human Resource Management*, Blackwell, Cambridge, MA

Bevan, S and Thompson, M (1991) Performance management at the cross-roads, *Personnel Management*, November, pp 36–39

Bitici, U S, Carrie, A S and McDevitt, L (1997) Integrate performance management systems: an audit and development goals, *TQM Magazine*, **9** (1), pp 46–53

Bowles, M L and Coates, G (1993) Image and substance: the management of performance as rhetoric or reality?, *Personnel Review*, **22** (2), pp 3–21

Boyett, J H and Conn, H P (1995) *Maximum Performance Management*, Glenbridge Publishing, Oxford

Brancato, C K (1995) *New Corporate Performance Measures*, Conference Board, New York

Campbell, J P (1990) Modelling the performance prediction problem in industrial and organizational psychology, in M P Dunnette and L M Hugh (eds), *Handbook of Industrial and Organizational Psychology*, Blackwell, Cambridge, MA

Cardy, R L and Dobbins, G H (1994) *Performance Appraisal: Alternative perspectives*, South-Western Publishing, Cincinnati, OH

Carlton, I and Sloman, M (1992) Performance appraisal in practice, *Human Resource Management Journal*, **2** (3), Spring, pp 80–94

Clayton, H (2004) How to perform under pressure, *People Management*, 29 July, pp 42–43

Cone, J W and Robinson, D G (2001) The power of performance, *TD*, August, pp 32–41

Daniels, A C (1987) What is PM?, *Performance Management*, July, pp 8–12

Drucker, P (1955) *The Practice of Management*, Heinemann, London

Earley, D C (1986) Computer-generated performance feedback in the magazine industry, *Organisation Behaviour and Human Decision Processes*, **41**, pp 50–64

Edwards, M R and Ewen, A T (1996) *360-Degree Feedback*, American Management Association, New York

Edwards, M R, Ewen, A T and O'Neal, S (1994) Using multi-source assessment to pay people not jobs, *ACA Journal*, Summer, pp 6–17

Engelmann, C H and Roesch, C H (1996) *Managing Individual Performance*, American Compensation Association, Scottsdale, AZ

Epstein, S and O'Brien, E J (1985) The person–situation debate in historical perspective, *Psychological Bulletin*, **83**, pp 956–74

Fisher, C M (1994) The difference between appraisal schemes: variation and acceptability – part 1, *Personnel Review*, **23** (8), pp 33–48

Fisher, M (1995) *Performance Appraisals*, Kogan Page, London

Flanagan, J C (1954) The critical incident technique, *Psychological Bulletin*, **51**, pp 327–58

Fletcher, C (1993) Appraisal: an idea whose time has gone?, *Personnel Management*, September, pp 34–37

Fowler, A (1990) Performance management: the MBO of the '90s?, *Personnel Management*, July, pp 47–54

Gannon, M (1995) Personal development planning, in M Walters (ed), *The Performance Management Handbook*, Institute of Personnel and Development, London

George, J (1986) Appraisal in the public sector: dispensing with the big stick, *Personnel Management*, May, pp 32–35

Goodridge, M (2001) The limits of performance management, *Topics 3*, ER Consultants, pp 23–28

Greenberg, R (2004) Beyond performance management: four principles of performance leadership, *Workspan*, September, pp 42–45

Guin, K A (1992) *Successfully Integrating Total Quality and Performance Appraisal*, Spring, Faulkner and Gray, New York

Hampson, S E (1982) *The Construction of Personality*, Routledge & Kegan Paul, London

Hartle, F (1995) *Transforming the Performance Management Process*, Kogan Page, London

Hendry, C, Bradley, P and Perkins, S (1997) Missed, *People Management*, 15 May, pp 20–25

Herzberg, F (1968) One more time: how do you motivate your employees?, *Harvard Business Review*, January–February, pp 109–20

Hobbs, N (2004) How to appraise board members, *People Management*, 20 May, pp 42–43

Humble, J (1972) *Management by Objectives*, Management Publications, London

Incomes Data Services (1997) *Performance Management*, IDS Study No. 626, Incomes Data Services, London

Industrial Society (1996) *Managing Best Practice: Rewarding performance*, Industrial Society, London

Institute of Personnel Management (1992) *Performance Management in the UK: An analysis of the issues*, Institute of Personnel Management, London

International Society for Performance Improvement (2004) Will employees perform better if you reward them?, *HR Focus*, December, pp 10–13

Jones, P *et al* (1995) Prisms of performance, *Ashridge Journal*, April, pp 10–14

Jones, T W (1995) Performance management in a changing context, *Human Resource Management*, Fall, pp 425–42

Kane, J S (1996) The conceptualisation and representation of total performance effectiveness, *Human Resource Management Review*, Summer, pp 123–45

Kaplan, R S and Norton, D P (1996) Strategic learning and the balanced scorecard, *Strategy and Leadership*, June, pp 20–34

Kaplan, R S and Norton, D P (1996) Using the balanced scorecard as a strategic management system, *Harvard Business Review*, January–February, pp 75–85

Kearns, P (2000) How do you measure up?, *Personnel Today*, 21 March, pp 21–22

Kermally, S (1997) *Managing Performance*, Butterworth-Heinemann, Oxford

Kessler, I and Purcell, J (1992) Performance-related pay: objectives and application, *Human Resource Management*, Spring, pp 16–33

Lampron, F and Koski, L (2004) Implementing web-enabled performance management, *Workspan*, January, pp 35–38

Latham, G P and Locke, E A (1979) Goal setting – a motivational technique that works, *Organisational Dynamics*, Autumn, pp 442–47

Lawler, E E (2003) Reward practices and reward system effectiveness, *Organizational Dynamics*, November, pp 396–404

Lawson, P (1995) Performance management: an overview, in M Walters (ed), *The Performance Handbook*, Institute of Personnel and Development, London

Lazer, R I and Wikstrom, W S (1977) *Appraising Managerial Performance: Current practices and new directions*, Conference Board, New York

Leventhal, G S (1980) What should be done with equity theory? New approaches to the study of fairness in social relationships, in K Gerken, M Greenberg and R Willis (eds), *Social Exchange: Advances in theory and research*, Plenum Press, New York

Levinson, H (1976) Appraisal of *what* performance?, *Harvard Business Review*, July–August, pp 30–46

Local Government Management Board (1995) *Guide to 360-Degree Feedback*, Local Government Management Board, London

Long, P (1986) *Performance Appraisal Revisited*, Institute of Personnel Management, London

McDonald, D and Smith, A (1991) A proven connection: performance management and business results, *Compensation and Benefits Review*, January–February, pp 59–64

Mackcay, I (1992) A *Manager's Guide to the Appraisal Discussion*, BACIE, London

Meisler, A (2003) Dead man's curve, *Workforce Management*, June, pp 44–49

Milkovich, G and Wigdor, A C (1991) *Pay for Performance: Evaluating performance appraisal and merit pay*, National Academy Press, Washington, DC

Murphy, K and Cleveland, J (1995) *Understanding Performance Appraisal*, Sage, London

Newton, T and Findlay, P (1996) Playing god? The performance of appraisal, *Human Resource Management Journal*, **6** (3), pp 42–56

Pedler, M, Burgoyne, J and Boydell, T (1986) *Manager's Guide to Self Development*, 2nd edn, McGraw-Hill, Maidenhead

Philpott, L and Sheppard, L (1992) Managing for improved performance, in M Armstrong (ed), *Strategies for Human Resource Management*, Kogan Page, London

Plachy, R J and Plachy, S J (1988) *Getting Results from Your Performance Management and Appraisal System*, AMACOM, New York

Porter, L W and Lawler, E E (1968) *Managerial Attitudes and Performance*, Irwin Dorsey, Homewood, IL

Randell, G H (1973) Performance appraisal: purpose, practices and conflicts, *Occupational Psychology*, **47**, pp 221–24

Robertson, I T, Smith, M and Cooper, C L (1992) *Motivation*, Institute of Personnel and Development, London

Rucci, A J, Kirn, S P and Quinn, R T (1998) The employee–customer–profit chain at Sears, *Harvard Business Review*, January–February, pp 82–97

Shneiderman, A M (1999) Why balanced score cards fail, *Journal of Strategic Performance Measurement*, January, pp 6–10

Sparrow, P (1996) Too good to be true, *People Management*, 5 December, pp 22–27

Stewart, V and Stewart, A (1982) *Managing the Poor Performer*, Gower, Aldershot

Stiles, P *et al* (1997) Performance management and the psychological contract, *Human Resource Management Journal*, **2** (1), pp 57–66

Storey, J (1985) The means of management control, *Sociology*, **19** (2), pp 193–212

Swanson, R A (1994) *Analysing for Improved Performance*, Berrett-Koehler, New York

Tamkin, P, Barber, L and Hirsh, W (1995) *Personal Development Plans: Case studies of practice*, Institute for Employment Studies, Brighton

Thomas, C (1995) Performance management, *Croner Pay and Benefits Bulletin*, August, pp 4–5

Thor, G G (1995) Using measurement to reinforce strategy, in H Rishner and C Fay (eds), *The Performance Imperative*, Jossey Bass, San Francisco

Townley, B (1990) A discriminating approach to appraisal, *Personnel Management*, December, pp 34–37

Townley, B (1990/91) Appraisal into UK universities, *Human Resource Management Journal*, **1** (2), pp 27–44 van de Vliet, A (1997) The new balancing card, *Management Today*, July, pp 78–79

Vaughan, S (2003) Performance: self as the principal evaluator, *Human Resource Development International*, September, pp 371–85

Walters, M (1995) Developing organisational measures, in M Walters (ed), *The Performance Management Handbook*, Institute of Personnel and Development, London

Wheatley, M (1996) How to score performance management, *Human Resources*, May–June, pp 24–26

Williams, S (1991) Strategy and objectives, in F Neale (ed), *The Handbook of Performance Management*, Institute of Personnel and Development, London

Willmore, J (2004) The future of performance, *Training and Development (USA)*, August, pp 26–31

Wingrove, C (2003) Developing an effective blend of process and technology in the new era of performance management, *Compensation and Benefits Review*, January–February, pp 25–31

Zigon, J (1994) Measuring the performance of work teams, *ACA Journal*, Autumn, pp 18–32

Author index

Subject index